CDL MINDED MARKETING

3-STEP SYSTEM TO **BUILD**, **ESTABLISH**, AND **GROW** YOUR BRAND IN **YOUR BUSINESS** FOR **ENTREPRENEURS**, **SMALL BUSINESS OWNERS**, AND COMMERCIAL **DRIVER/OPERATORS**

JOE RYDER

Copyright © 2021 by Joe Ryder.

All rights reserved.

The content contained within this book may not be reproduced, duplicated, or transmitted without direct written permission from the author or the publisher. Under no circumstances will any blame or legal responsibility be held against the publisher, or author, for any damages, reparation, or monetary loss due to the information contained within this book, either directly or indirectly.

Legal Notice:
This book is copyright protected. It is only for personal use. You cannot amend, distribute, sell, use, quote or paraphrase any part, or the content within this book, without the consent of the author or publisher.

Disclaimer Notice:
Please note that the information contained within this document is for educational and entertainment purposes only. All effort has been executed to present accurate, up to date, reliable, complete information. No warranties of any kind are declared or implied. Readers acknowledge that the author is not engaged in rendering legal, financial, medical, or professional advice. The content within this book has been derived from various sources. Please consult a licensed professional before attempting any techniques outlined in this book.

By reading this document, the reader agrees that under no circumstances is the author responsible for any losses, direct or indirect, that are incurred as a result of the use of the information contained within this document, including, but not limited to, errors, omissions, or inaccuracies.

Printed in the United States of America.

Cover Design by 100Covers.com
Interior Design by FormattedBooks.com

TABLE OF CONTENTS

Introduction vii

Glossary of Marketing Terms xiii

Chapter One: Strategy Will Win Over the Most
    Challenging of Circumstances. 1

Chapter Two: The 9 Effective Necessities for Your
    Marketing Strategy 14

Chapter Three: Covering All the Bases 32

Chapter Four: Building Your CDL Brand Step One - Know
    Yourself, Know Your Audience 54

Chapter Five: Building Your CDL Brand Step Two -
    Incentives, Referrals, and Loyalty Programs 84

Chapter Six: Building Your CDL Brand Step Three -
    Reach Your Clients and Grow Your Business 99

Chapter Seven: Your Successful Launch 113

Additional Information, Helpful Industry Links, Suggested
    Reading 121

Suggested Reading 151

References 153

Special Bonus Offer: Free Gift for You! :)

Thank you! Here's a Free Gift! For You :)

As a special thanks from me to you, you'll receive:

- ❏ 3 Powerful Elements of Productivity in your Business
- ❏ 5 Simple Strategies to Mastering Productivity in your Business
- ❏ The Highest Quality of Productivity Charts
- ❏ Valuable Resources that you Must Know and much more!

To receive your Free copy of the CDL Business Productivity GAME PLAN, you can go to my website at:
cdlforlife.com/cdl-business-resources

SCAN ME   **SCAN ME**
(For your Free Business Game Plan)   (If you want my Books for Free)

Also If you would like to get my books for Free and before anyone else, go to my website at:
cdlforlife.com/cdl-business-resources

INTRODUCTION

> *"I'm convinced that about half of what separates successful entrepreneurs from the non-successful ones is pure perseverance."*
> —*Steve Jobs*

When did you first believe you wanted to be an entrepreneur?

Have you known it your whole life, or did a certain experience lure you into the world of trucking?

All of us know, the trucking lifestyle isn't easy, so it certainly wasn't because you wanted to put in your 14 hours on the road and then kick back for a 6-hour nap, only to get up and do it all again.

Something inside your heart and perhaps a force inside your soul called you to pursue this occupation and this way of life. Some even refer to it as a 'calling' they feel when they get in the cab and face the open road. But it doesn't stop there.

You know how to maneuver a quarter ton 'box of bricks' in the tightest of dock areas; you can sleep at any time of the day; and you can navigate a big city with your eyes closed.

JOE RYDER

There's a certain way of thinking and 'feeling' which is in every driver's blood; it's there when you schedule a long haul and it's there when you finally get a shower after a 4-day run. It's there when you're driving in the morning with the whole world out in front of you just waiting to be experienced, and it's there when you are on the dark, quiet highway, in the middle of nowhere, wondering what your family and friends are doing.

And now, you've decided to drive for yourself. The industry is second nature to you now and you feel you're ready to offer customers something new, something improved, or maybe it's just that you want to improve *your* life—be your own boss, manage a skilled team, with new ideas and a new set of rules for operating a business.

When it comes to setting up a successful company, there are basics which need to be in place, decisions that have to be made.

Do you want to cover just a specific region?

Are you going to cater to a targeted industry, such as livestock or refrigeration?

Do you have nimble trucks which will only deliver within city blocks, or are you an expert at managing double and triple trailers for interstate loads?

Or are you wanting the entire pie, covering every specialty imaginable so you can get as many trips scheduled as possible?

When considering all the possibilities and commitments, it's easy to feel overwhelmed. Not only do you want to satisfy your customers, but you should be in it to improve your life too, whether by making more money, being able to govern your own schedule, or moving into management and having your own crew of drivers.

Within these pages are the nuggets you'll need to begin your profitable CDL/trucking business. The methods will help you to discover your focus and will lead you to choosing your branding strategy, which, if done correctly, will lead into a marketing strategy that you will custom fit for your business. After you have picked the marketing channels that not only find most comfortable with, but that will give you the results you are looking for, your marketing strategy will be set and finding your ideal customers will just be a matter of putting the strategy in motion.

You'll write your business' mission/vision statement, declaring the foundational values you'll build your company on. You will also find that having your mission statement close at hand can be a reminder of what you wanted your company to stand for and why you started it in the first place. There will be times which may challenge you and you'll be ready to junk the whole idea; having this statement close at hand can pull you back to basics and give you the reasons you need to rethink your future and move forward.

After you have written your mission and vision statements, it's time to assemble a business plan. This process has many components, and we'll guide you through the process as you learn the important role your business plan plays when organizing your company, and, when it's time, designing your marketing brand. It has a key role in the building of your company.

When you've laid the groundwork for your business and you're ready to move forward with devising a marketing plan, we'll discuss all the tools you can use, which will make finding your ideal customer easy. The process of getting your company in front of these businesses is paramount in catching their attention and eventually turning them into life-long customers will be explained with sample situations and understandable terms. It isn't as mysterious or unattainable as it might seem right now.

All strategies and channels you can use are taught in an easy-to-understand language, so you don't have to worry about being experienced in the field or having done it before. It also isn't grade-school dummied-down. When you finish, you'll wonder why you've been so apprehensive for so long. It can be easy!

The world of traditional and online advertising will open doors you had no idea existed, blending a couple of channels for a simple strategy to get your first customers, right up to a multi-launch campaign. The process is easy, and as you build your company image and develop ways to reach your customers, you will quickly gain the ability and know-how to mix TV ads with PPC promotions or blog postings with Facebook ads. The best part? You'll know exactly why you're combining each channel and for what intended outcome.

Finally, the ominous task of designing and launching a website will be simplified and explained, firstly with the benefits of how an informational site can almost run your business for you, and secondly, how easy it is to assemble and launch with a few knowledgeable tricks and your own computer or laptop.

When you finish this book, all the tools you'll need to begin your business strategy, from choosing how to develop a company logo to building loyal customer relationships, will be in your marketing strategy toolbox, and it will all be as simple to set into motion as counting to 3.

GLOSSARY OF MARKETING TERMS

Advertising - any means by which a business draws attention to potential customers for sales.

Affiliate marketing - a process where two people or businesses have an agreement to promote a product or service to their existing customers. If a recipient purchases a product or service, the promoter receives a percentage of the sale.

Blogging - typically, an online (usually recurring) journal entry or article of interest regarding a person's experience or opinion.

Campaign - a marketing blitz using multiple media tools to achieve an intended outcome.

Channel - a marketing method which uses optimal marketing options to achieve a preferred end result.

Customer awareness - recognition of a business, practice, or initiative within a community or industry by its customers.

Market presence - recognition of a business within its industry.

Multimedia - a combination of media that utilizes traditional and non-traditional methods, such as printed flyers, radio spots, Facebook ads, and website blogs.

Niche - a specific segment within an industry, having unique characteristics and nuances; can be defined as a purchaser demographic who would benefit the most from an offer.

PPC (pay per click) - an advertising tool used in online marketing, by which an established website sells ad space to a buyer and the buyer only pays if a viewer 'clicks' on their ad, which takes them to a promotional or landing page.

Promotions - a specific advertising strategy with a purpose to achieve sales.

Public relations - a method of promoting a company to community and civic groups and creating a network of common interest groups.

Strategy - an organized, long-term plan assembled with a specific goal in mind.

Social media - the industry as a whole, consisting of social sites such as Facebook, Twitter, etc., where members can interact and post media to theirs and other member pages.

Social networking - creating communication between people connecting on the Internet, usually with a common idea or goal.

Website - a location on the Internet where a person or business can present ideas, products, or services for others to view and interact with.

CHAPTER ONE

Strategy Will Win Over the Most Challenging of Circumstances

As with any plan, putting your brand and marketing strategy together can seem overwhelming.

Don't let this intimidate you. The glossary in the front of this book is for your reference of the most common and often-used terms in business, marketing, advertising, and branding.

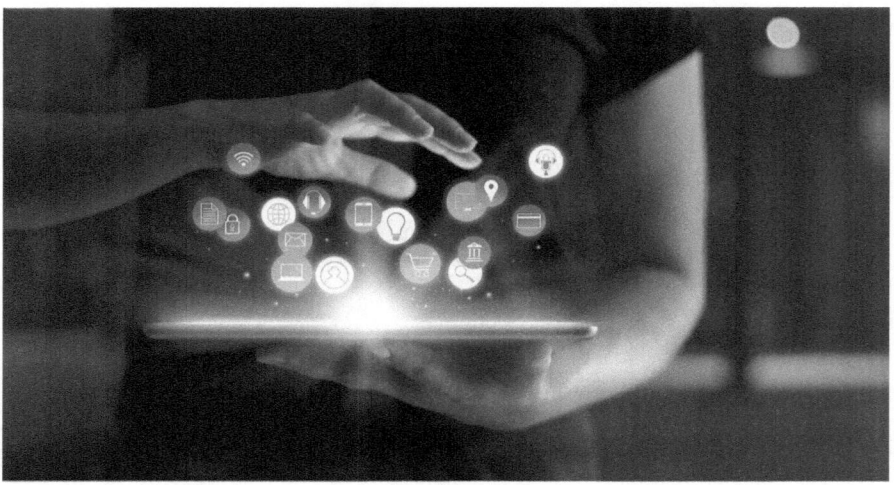

Starting your own business is a challenge, but you know your industry, you know what is needed behind the scenes to be successful. You also know that you can do this if you have the answers to, not only some, but to *all* of your questions. By discussing where our industry is now and some of our advantages and set-backs, a clearer image may give way to how quickly things change and how adapting to recent events can launch you in a direction you may not be aware of.

As 2020 began, the trucking industry was growing and had a lot of competition. Now, as we begin the second half of the year, even more people have taken up the idea to start their own companies.

New customers are in need of transportation services who used other forms before the COVID-19 pandemic broke out. Many foundational industries, particularly retail and manufacturing, have used truck transportation exclusively and have found air transport to be affordable. Due to the fact that airlines are trying to make up lost revenue from clientele, many corporations have closed their businesses, rates have dropped and therefore truckers have lost their businesses and their clients. Still, other trucking lines have lost their revenue completely, even in the trade show markets, the esteemed and long-term clients have turned into ghosts, and are now trying to figure out new avenues and industries for themselves.

Everyone is maneuvering to make money where it's been lost, and as transportation professionals are in a bind trying to come up with solutions, we are the last line of defense to see who is in need and who is not.

But one thing is very clear:

The nation and the world needs CDL Minded professionals in the CDL industry.

Products and services will still have to move from one place to another.

And now, you believe you can offer these new (and previous) customers, new choices. So, let's get down to business and begin to build your company!

Assess Your Skills

- What do you do best?

- What can you offer that the 'other company' does not?

- Are your prices better?

- Do you guarantee your arrival dates?

- Are you a master at moving produce, steel machinery, or some other specialty you feel needs more attention?

Know Your Strengths and Your Weaknesses

- Do you like to crunch numbers and feel you're a natural in financial matters?

- Does building a website or social presence intimidate you?

- What things do you do that people compliment you on, or tell others to get in touch with you for?

- Does the thought of recording a video scare the living daylights out of you, or do you think it would be fun to develop a personality in your market and gather a following of like-minded customers?

Weigh the Specifics of Your Business and What You Want to Accomplish

- Do you have a goal in mind, like running goods for food shelters or delivering donations for Habitat for Humanity?

- Are you focused on having more money in the bank to help your family?

- Will having a stable client base give you the stability you're looking for in a world turned upside down?

CDL MINDED MARKETING

After you've developed the basis of your business and know the ins and outs of moving forward, it's time to assemble the basics for building and running a successful company. By thinking of yourself as a 'business,' you have started the process of having a 'business mindset' which needs to be in place before building your image, or 'brand,' for marketing.

Getting in now with a new business or taking steps to further improve your existing company couldn't have come at a better time, believe it or not. A well-thought-out business strategy can sustainably work now, and also in the future.

Once you have listed your best skills, decide specifically on what you want to offer and have a good idea of who you want to offer it to; the rest will just be decisions and action. Ask yourself the following three questions:

1. How much money do you want to invest?

2. How many people will you have to reach in order for your business to be profitable?

3. How can you set up a campaign which will govern itself and only need occasional maintenance if you're on the road or want to take time off?

These considerations are part of the overall structure of your business framework. Your next steps in constructing a solvent business should include:

Writing a Business Plan - The old proverb still makes sense; if you don't know where you are going, how will you know when you get there? The same logic rings true for starting a business. Organize your thoughts. In *Step 1 of Building Your Brand*, you'll go through this process. There are specifics you'll want to make sure are set in stone, but others you may not be sure of, or even if they will be part of your plan. Don't worry—we'll get you there.

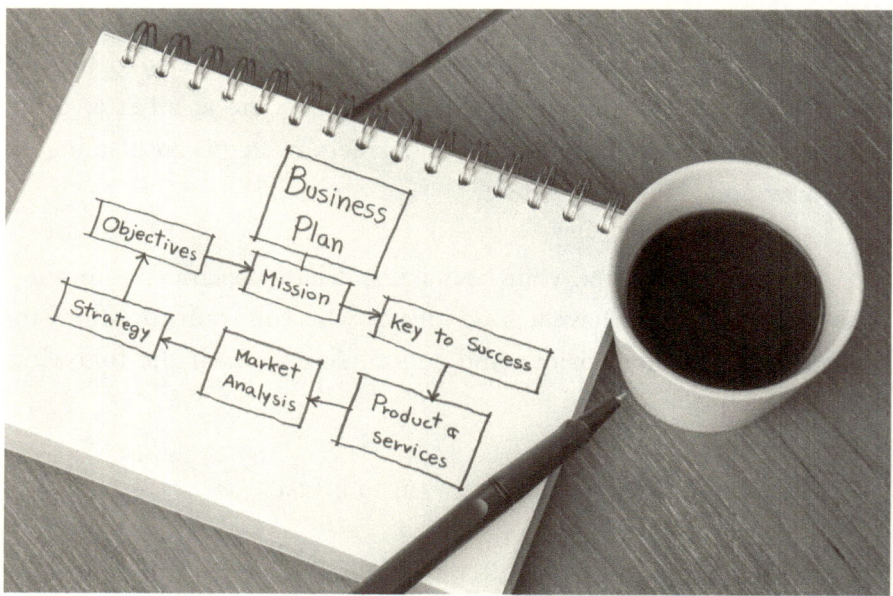

Establish Your Business, Legally - By implementing a Limited Liability Company, sole proprietorship, or corporation, you will be setting boundaries for your company and protecting yourself from liability or disastrous events. You will learn how each one works, the benefits and downfalls, and choose which structure will work best for you. Discussions later will include establishing a registered agent (not having one can jeopardize your business' operations by missing state mandate notices, tax documents, legal notices, or wage garnishments if you become distracted or forget to file). You'll learn why you should apply for an electronic identification number (EIN) for your business, which is required for you to open a banking account and will also be used on all tax identification for the life of your business. You'll learn about shareholders, partners, personal and business assets, and more. Protect your business, protect yourself.

Purchase and Possess All Business Licenses and Permits - Check with the state your office will reside in, and also any states you will be traveling to within your territory. In addition to the specific business license(s) you may need, you must also retain:

> *Commercial Driver's License* (CDL) and any endorsements which may be needed - it is a Federal Law to have this.

> *Motor Carrier Operating Authority number* - you may need more than one of these numbers for your business, depending on your specific operations.

> *USDOT Number* - to identify all motor carriers when they conduct inspections, investigations or audits, the Federal Motor Carrier Safety Administration (FMCSA) uses a USDOT number, an assigned and unique number for each company.

> *International Registration Plan (IRP) credentials and an International Fuel Tax Agreement (IFTA) decal* - if you operate in multiple states, you will need to obtain both of these credentials to be compliant.

Choose to Buy or Lease Your Equipment - Make sure your equipment can handle the freight you intend on delivering. When you are starting out, consider whether buying or leasing will suit your operation best.

Document Your Income and Expenses - There are numerous software programs which can make this task easy and also offer the needed reports to submit with payroll and tax claims. Choose one which will organize your entries best for a clear and understandable summary. Pick one you understand and can use easily, because you will be using it every day. Due to the many times your entry amounts and receipts are received at untimely rates, sometimes weeks and months after a delivery has been completed, it is important that this tool is as uncomplicated and user-friendly as possible.

Often, an accountant familiar with a trucking company's operation can start you off with the right tools and suggest the best way for you to handle your accounts. Having this advice can save you headaches down the road if you've used a complicated or non-compliant software, or have to re-count 6 months worth of entries.

Establish the way you'll be paid by your customers before you begin scheduling too, so both you and your clients are on the same page when you begin. Maintain complete records of all expenses before, during, and after the delivery. Keep personal and business expenses separated.

Purchase Appropriate Insurance - Compare pricing and make sure you have all areas covered, including primary liability, physical damage, passenger accident, and cargo insurance. Have several agents bid on your needs to get the best coverage at the appropriate rate.

Stay in Compliance - You will have many time-sensitive and filing requirements to apply for and submit. Failure to do any of these in an untimely manner may cost you good standing, delinquent fees, and perhaps even revoke your legal status of operation. Keeping your required reports, licenses, and permits all in order is a must; find a management system to help you stay on top of these and all document submissions in a timely fashion.

Finding Customers to Help You Grow Your Business - Though the use of load boards can get you immediate deliveries, and word of mouth works if you spend time conversing with many people, the best way to make money and have a thriving trucking company is to have a marketing strategy which is aimed at your audience. Learn the tools presented here, and you'll be a master at your own success for as long as you own your business.

Learn and Build a Marketing Strategy - You are in the right place to learn these techniques and design your path for a successful and profitable CDL operating company. But first things first. Before we begin with marketing methods and how you'll gain customers and business, some foundational concepts need to be in place in order for the strategies to make sense.

Trucking companies are unique in many ways. Our hours are different from most other businesses. We comply with federal regulations for times driving and time off. We have hours and hours of training and learning our rigs. We read, drive, listen, test, apply, and submit more paperwork than a college student applying for loans.

We drive in the day, we drive at night, we drive in the ice, sleet, rain, snow, and we drive in the fog. We even drive in temperatures over 100F degrees. We work up to 70 hours in an eight-day week, but have to make sure we don't drive longer than 11 hours straight. Most days we drive over 500 miles.

So what is so appealing about being a truck driver?

Well, each of us has our own definition and reason, but living the same lifestyle with other like-minded people who live by these standards brings comradery and understanding to the job. Some do it for life, some get in and get out, and some drivers never feel at home unless they are headed down the road to the unknown, stretched out and unforeseen, in front of them.

My point being, we are a different breed. We understand each other, though we know each of us is unique and different.

And then there are those of us who want to run a business.

We are, yet again, another segmented and divided group. But we have our ideas and we have our dreams. The first of which is to be our own boss.

You already know the trucking life and how it unfolds. Here, you will move from behind the wheel, frustrated, to being in front of your goals, which is success. Our industry is tough and not everyone could handle its ups and downs. But when you own your own trucking business, you are in charge and you are the boss.

Let's identify the areas which prove to be the most challenging in the CDL industry today, before beginning the marketing structure or methodology.

We'll outline several concerns and how to react, respond, and maneuver through these problems, so you can see how to identify the actual need, develop several ways to solve the problem, and then choose the best solution for your particular circumstance.

The trucking industry has been hit hard by environmental concerns, fluctuating fuel costs, driver shortages, trucking regulations, safety concerns, and now the COVID-19 pandemic. Each of these set-backs are out of the trucker's reach to solve. However, the best thing we can do is to be proactive and address each of them, depending on how closely they are related to your particular business.

Environmental Concerns - What can you do to lessen the impact of your driving on the environment? Make it part of your campaign if it's necessary to your customers. Also, be aware of your surroundings; people outside our circle are watching us carefully. Again, by being proactive, you can disarm confrontations, both direct and indirect, by recycling when possible, taking precautions with the environment, and being respectful of others' point of views.

Fluctuating Fuel Costs - Because the fuel industry has been pulled into politics and its roller coaster ride of power, being a business owner with a budget to predict is somewhat of a guessing game. If you can average on the higher side and still maintain a lucrative strategy, do it. If not, govern your best bet on the average cost over a period of time (2 years, 5 years, 10 years). This may be an area you will have to monitor closely. Keeping a prudent eye on the current costs can prevent losses down the road. And always buy fuel based on the cheapest *base price*, not pump price!

Driver Shortages - Hiring experienced drivers to work for you can be the most expensive challenge of your business. It can also give you the best rewards. If you have the time to hold out for the stellar drivers, of course, do. But often, independent drivers are hired to just get a commitment delivered to keep the customer. If possible, always keep the communication open with all drivers. If there is anyone who may know the good and bad points of a driver, it's a fellow driver.

Trucking Regulations and Toll Charges - There are several ways regulations and toll charges are calculated. As an operator, you need to be aware of these regulations before conducting charges for your services, as tolls and regulations change often, especially if you drive through more states or countries than your own. Passes are usually the easiest way to take care of business, but as you know, there are several places where weigh stations and individual tolls can be charged. Some charge by axle count, others by size of your rig, some even charge with a combination of the two, such as the New York State Thoroughfare. Stay up-to-date on these fees, particularly when quoting bids, and you will cover yourself when it comes time to pay up.

Safety Concerns - These are rules of the road and have steep penalties if not abided by. Being the owner, you are walking a fine line between taking care of your drivers and getting shipments delivered on time. Rule of thumb, always err on the safety of your driver and staying within restriction codes. They are there for a reason.

According to the Census of Fatal Occupational Injuries, 2019, heavy tractor-trailer truck drivers had the highest fatality rate (831 of 966 in Transportation Fatalities[3]) of any other occupation. Occupational Safety and Health Administration (OSHA) has strict regulations in place because of this consistent statistic, and others which are even more alarming, which rank CDL operators as *the highest risk occupation for injury*. Keep yourself and your drivers safe to the best of your abilities, as well as everyone else on the road; know the regulations and abide by them.

High Cost of Load Boards - There will always be the chance you will have an empty truck and need to go to a load board to find a load. But keep this practice to a minimum. Deal directly with the shipper whenever possible, as brokers retain anywhere from 10% to 25% of the load price. The obvious reason is very understandable, but remember, it costs you money in the long run.

COVID-19 - Transportation is always at the call of demand, and when revenues shut down, so does the trucking industry. Now is a hard time to begin a trucking company, but it's not impossible if you design your niche with knowledge. By planning well, choosing your developments wisely, and making sure you aren't over-spending or under-delivering, you will outlast the companies who are dropping their fundamentals to stay on the road. Keep to your commitment of your brand, your business image, and you will attract like-minded and CDL Minded customers that will appreciate your customer care and your honesty.

Because the trucking industry promises such plentiful business returns (profits), many have invested who know little about its personality. Putting together a smart and stable business plan then pursuing a savvy and responsive marketing strategy will not only serve you well in establishing yourself within the industry, but if done right, it will sustain you in the coming months and years.

All challenges are solvable; what looks big without knowledge becomes child's play when the secrets are known. Dig in and master the skills. The basis of developing a plan to move forward is to know what you are moving forward *with*.

In the next chapter you will learn how to develop a strategy for your company and the importance of having it in place.

CHAPTER TWO

The 9 Effective Necessities for Your Marketing Strategy

The hopes you have for your business carries great power when assembling your business plan and strategizing a marketing campaign.

This is only the beginning, however. Building a successful marketing strategy depends on mastering a few simple ideas. Namely, knowing exactly what your business focus is and who is your ideal customer. You need to be steadfast on the identity of your company and what you will offer before you can extend those services to customers and clients. Being clear doesn't mean being broad-minded, so narrow it down. Instead of saying 'We deliver farm-grown produce to local markets and independent grocers' try 'By specializing in organically farmed produce, our standards for delivery are as high as your standards are for growing.' By stating specifics, you draw in the customers who are passionate about their product. The more specialized the client's product, the more passionate they are about it, and they will try to do business with the same type of people.

What Market Are You Going to Provide Service To?

We've touched on this previously, but now you need to drill it down and decide exactly who your clients will be. If you are still wondering what industry you want to provide service to, or thinking you'll just open your doors and see who walks in, your marketing and any other investment to attain customers will be expensive and it will fail miserably. If you don't have a clear voice to speak directly to your client, they will never hear your message. If this is the case, chances are they will hear the message of your competitor.

Once you have determined the industry which will be your focus, you need to put yourself in your potential customers 'shoes' and discover who they are and what they are passionate about.

What Problems Do Your Customers Have?

Not only do you have to understand who they are and what they are passionate about, but you need to identify any needs, pains, or problems they may have. Imagine yourself as a business owner in their company. What would you be concerned with? What problems do you have that you wish would be solved?

By being the answer to their grief and problems, you will rise on a pedestal, and they will come to you time and time again.

So, if you've identified their needs and possible problems, where do you go from there?

Produce a marketing message which asks them about their problem. For example:

"Are you experiencing consistently late deliveries by your trucking firm?"

Then solve the problem:

"We guarantee every delivery is on time and on budget."

A guarantee is a binding promise, so remember, when solving their problem, don't over-commit. If you can't do it, don't say you can.

Maybe you could bring it down a notch:

"If a delivery is late, the next shipment is 50% off!"

Perhaps your potential customer has trouble finding trucks to deliver their product quickly, or perhaps they need pick-up times within 24 hours. You could advertise:

"Full fleet of delivery trucks to provide immediate pick-up."

If a client needs custom trailer packing because of delicate equipment, you could state:

"We offer on-site personal loading, to your specifications."

How Can You Solve Those Needs or Problems?

This is why you are in business; to help others and provide a product or service. You know these answers. It's why you have the desire to thrive in your own business. If you develop a strategy which will catch your customers' attention by identifying their problems, provide solutions to those problems, and make the process of getting that solution easy, effective, and productive, you are well on your way to building a clientele who will be loyal and engaging customers for life.

Now, let's get down to specifics. Here are the ways to get your marketing strategy moving forward.

9 Effective Necessities for Your Marketing Strategy

1) Stand out from your competition by portraying a unique business advantage in your niche.

You have your own style and way of doing things. Though each of us are different and handle situations uniquely, in business we are attracted to those who tend to think and approach our livelihoods similarly. In other words, we trust someone who we feel connected to intuitively rather than someone we don't quite understand or value.

Stay clear in your message and keep it simple. Don't be afraid to show your clients who you are and what your business stands for. Like-minded clients will notice and will be easier to win over.

There will always be people who don't see the world the same way as you. And this is fine, as you won't be able to please everyone all the time. Focus on the customers and clients who do matter, who do value your work ethic and appreciate what you have to offer. Keeping these companies well attended to and satisfied will keep you busy enough without worrying why another company didn't sign on with you. There are always wonderful customers out there who are looking for you and hoping you can help them with their needs.

2) Build a good, reliable reputation.

A good reputation is priceless and takes time to build. The sooner you show your business integrity and how you approach problems and solutions, the sooner you will establish yourself and develop credibility in your industry. Word spreads, especially if you turned a bad situation into a quick solution. Share your experiences in your marketing strategy too (on your website and as customer testimonials, discussed in further detail in Chapter 6). The more you show how dependable, trustworthy, and reliable you are, the quicker your customers will share their positive experiences, and your client base will grow at a lively pace.

Independent truck companies are at a disadvantage when it comes to public images. Yes, we are seen as being professional drivers and most people admire our skills and courtesy. But sometimes our good value gets lost in the race, and even we begin to question if we are capable of handling the stress or question if we are giving good service.

Take the initiative and be the best you can be. Self-respect is a big motivator and can get you through the darkest of times. When you work independently, we all know, you can come across hard times now and again. When you know you are doing a good job, the best job you can, and you are providing a great service to your customers and their businesses, you can cross insecurity and doubt right off the list.

And if you find yourself questioning your abilities or direction, realize where you are now doesn't necessarily mean you will be there next year, 5 years from now, or even at retirement age. You have the means to create greatness.

Stay away from temptations which can defeat your intentions. Keep a clean record free of drug, alcohol, or accident-related incidents. Pursue good routes, growth opportunities, and higher expectations from your business. By setting the bar just a bit higher, you can reach the goal and move toward the next one with more ease and incentive.

3) Maximize visibility.

Within the industry of CDL operators, there are thousands of different types of hauling. Using a multiple-faceted marketing strategy can help you reach all of your potential clients for your specific business. You may have clients who are on the internet for most of their day, while another client is on the phone or traveling between cities. To reach each of these potential clients, you must first determine where they spend their time, and, secondly, what marketing tool you need to use to best reach and communicate with each one.

The first and foremost hub of your market presence is to have a current and updated website. It's your calling card, information sheet, personal secretary, and talent list all rolled into one. In today's world, without one, you are invisible to your clients, without credibility and without information. You will find out how to launch the easiest of sites with the best information stated, announcing you are open and ready for business. Look to the later chapters to achieve this task, and no, it really isn't as daunting as it sounds.

Make sure your image comes off in a professional manner also. Being a professional entrepreneur takes strength and agility, not to mention patience and diligence. By showing you are a business owner who commands all these traits, you will draw the same level of professionalism in your clientele. You won't be dealing with hustlers or companies who undercut your bids or devalue your service. By portraying the image of a business professional you want to work with, you will attract and retain great customers and like-minded, responsible companies. No one wants to work with half-rate businesses and agents who don't 'deliver' on what they promise.

4) Develop customer relationships.

As much as this seems like a given, more often than not business owners get caught up in the day-to-day operations and fail to acknowledge their potential and existing customers. When building your client base, take more time to get to know the people who are reading your website, answering your posts, commenting on your social media, or asking questions on the phone. Become interested in them, and they will see you in a different and positive light.

Your existing clients need attention in this way too. Keep them feeling like they are as important five years down the road as they were the day they signed their first contract. Stay engaged, ask about new directions they are taking and how you can make the process easier for them. Each client will handle the communication differently, so having several avenues to connect (email, messaging, phone calls, etc.) provides a better chance for keeping and maintaining a great relationship with them. By offering many ways to connect, you are also making it easier for them to be in touch with you, as well as providing more opportunity for the relationship to develop with trust and loyalty.

Also, take care to keep the lines of communication open, and always welcome their input and views. Even if you have a client who seems like they don't wish to speak with you, stay in contact. Send them your newsletter once a month or keep them on your promotions list to receive your latest discounts. You never know when they will need you, which may depend on either a rush transport across town, or an emergency haul across the country. If you are on their radar when the moment arises, chances are they will give you a try. Just because you don't hear from a customer doesn't mean they aren't listening.

5) Maintain a level playing field, whether you are a large company or a single-person operation.

In today's marketing world, you can be large or small, specific or broad. By strategizing your marketing to reach your specific customers and give them exactly what they are in need of, you have accomplished the main objective. Do you have to knock on a million doors to land that one big account?

No, all you have to do is find out where they 'are' (interests, commonalities, demographics), why they are there, and create relatable messaging to 'speak' to them personally. Your image can be as big or as small as you choose, especially when conversing online. The internet gives you any number of ways to project your brand and gain trust. If done correctly, you can win out over large competition, time and time again, by focusing your personal service, offering customized care, and building an engaged network.

You also offer something the large companies and corporations can't offer, and that is 'the personal touch.' If a client feels they have your attention and is confident you will do everything in your power to get them what they need, they will return this customized attention back to you with continued business and word-of-mouth praise.

Large companies may offer customer service or have staff waiting at the end of a phone line to take calls, but what a business owner who is having you move their product wants is to know how that person views their product, will safety for their shipment be at risk, or will the driver be rude to the receiving dock, who you know, is a bit of a *tough old dog*. You already know, the large companies do have their great drivers, some of them have all great drivers. But as a client in a large pool of businesses, it is pretty much a given that you won't have the same driver each time, and you won't be able to connect with them like you can with the customized and care-driven trucking business.

Never underestimate the power of being a personalized and helpful operator. Everyone wants to know someone has their back and won't shortcut their promise. Large companies don't neglect their customers intentionally, but at some point their customers do feel like they are just a number in the system. And that suits many businesses, but these aren't your customers; this isn't the world where you will shine.

We all would much rather have a personal connection with our business partners than be an order number at the end of the day. Take advantage of this, listen to your customer, ask questions to make sure you understand their business and their needs. Then deliver the best possible service you can provide, all with a couple of preliminary conversations and a sincere 'thank you' after the job is completed. There isn't a bad or weak spot in this scenario at all. By being an attentive and supportive supplier, you will possess their devotion time and time again.

5) Achieve a high return on your investment.

In today's marketing world, you can spend hundreds and thousands of dollars on marketing techniques and ad campaigns. But, you can also spend your dollars wisely (or take advantage of many directives which are free or cost next to nothing to use) and attain just as much as those expensive and hit-and-miss blanket campaigns.

By focusing on a specific niche, industry, product, or service, you can get the attention of your intended audience easily, make your offer, and gain new business quickly and easily, all while doing what comes easiest for you and providing exactly the service needed for your customer. Your potential clients are intelligent and savvy; they know what they want and when they see you offer that exact thing, they will engage with you quickly and become faithful followers. The power of placing yourself in front of their eyes has never been easier, and creating a brand and presence in the places where your clients will be found can be inexpensive and lucrative.

In addition to narrowing down your audience target to the exact audience you want as ideal customers, it's wise to offer them more value than what they initially want. By being the best business owner you can be, you will give them the confidence of knowing you are top-notch in every area of your industry. This includes:

- Being current and up-to-date on your permits, licenses, insurance, and regulations.

- Always looking for innovative and cost-effective ways to save money, not only for your business, but for your customer too.

- Staying current and possibly even a leader in furthering your education; this gives you the knowledge you'll need to incorporate new techniques into your business.

- Have back-up plans in case of emergencies and keep a watchful eye on economic downturns by evaluating the effect they may have on your industry and business.

- Always be aware of your competition's strategies and tactics; stay one step ahead of them with your own techniques and offers if possible.

In other words, be the exceptional operator.

When you know what is going on in the world around you, you can speculate, plan, and prepare for good and bad times, and you will have the satisfaction and knowledge that you will always be there for your company and its success, as well as your customers and their ever-changing needs.

6) Lower marketing and operating costs.

Your own sector of industry, or niche, can give you many options to reach your clients, and quite often they are very specific. Online advertising can give you the options you want at minimal costs, sometimes even free!

Maybe you are a milk tanker line, and you are trying to reach independent dairies. How do you reach those rural people with your company benefits of 24/7 hourly truck availability or scheduled routine customized routes for the latest in dairy transport?

First, where are these dairy farmers in terms of managing their own business? Most currently have multiple dairies and many employees, and being small as a single dairy farmer just isn't feasible any longer. Where is the decision maker to be found? They probably check the price of goods each day (online, which means you might want to run a banner ad on popular investment sites) or perhaps merchandise which the farmer may need (a banner ad on milking machine sites or bovine vet care). Many of these ads can be set up as a rotating ad, and you only pay for each 'click' or time a person checks out your page or site (pay per click, or PPC). Today's options couldn't align better with the small business CDL trucker.

Can you see how and where your money will do the most good? When you use an approach of segment influence, you can reach even the most elusive of customers. As you become more educated about your niche, you'll also be able to see how analysis reports will give you the answers you are in need of when a campaign doesn't quite give you what you were looking for, or what words will turn a warm response to your ad into an explosive one.

It's also a good idea to stay up on your driving requirements and keep a clean record. By being in good standing with all the agencies, state, and federal mandates, it shows that you're responsible and you handle your business in a professional manner. These things are vitally important to customers. If you have savvy and responsible customers yourself, as you are hoping to acquire, they will check to make sure your business is an operation that they'll want to transport their goods. If you have a poor standing within your industry, your potential customers will find someone else to move their product.

7) Establish yourself as an innovator.

Chances are, one of the reasons you want to own your own business is that you want to improve something or offer an alternative. You've taken the first step, but don't stop there.

By showing your ability to adapt, to handle emergencies, and to move forward with smart solutions and ideas, you will also catch the attention of customers and build rapport as a company which can handle the tough stuff. There are so many ways a CDL operator can be tripped up by outside forces. Show your customers you can handle yourself under pressure, and you've won their faith for unexpected but inevitable challenges.

Always keep up on trends and changes in the industry too. If there is a way to improve driving techniques or expand the services you offer, evaluate the options and see if they may benefit you.

Along the way of keeping up-to-date, employing changes to stay on top of your business, and showing professionalism in stressful times, make sure you recognize yourself for the valuable and resourceful person that you are. Without initiative, without incentive, and without applied knowledge, your business would fold in the turn of a wheel. Your self-worth and confidence is what keeps your business making money and your truck(s) on the road. Congratulate yourself for the steps you've taken to get to your higher ground. No one else could have done this quite like you have—be proud of your achievements and motivation.

8) Initiate, communicate, listen, and engage.

Always remember to take advantage of connecting with potential and established customers. In today's world, everyone is accustomed to being social and having acquaintances. 'Likes' are valued on Facebook just as much as the number of connections on LinkedIn. It is also very demanding. If we don't like what we are seeing or who we are working with, we simply detach and find another outlet.

Your business will be no different. If someone is feeling abandoned or neglected (and it probably will happen over the lifetime of your company), they will take their marbles and leave the game. On the other hand, you may very well be the game they decide to join if disappointments have occurred with another company. Even if you aren't the 'chatty' type, find someone who is and put them in charge of your customer relations. Establishing and maintaining a vigilant connection, whether your clients answer back or not is essential to running and building a successful business in today's world.

Always be there to answer questions and offer help. Make sure you communicate within a business day's passing, if only to say you are away from your desk but will be back in touch when you are able. If you don't know the answer, don't pretend that you do. Nothing shows worse than someone trying to be something they aren't. Tell them you don't know, but you will find the answer and be right back with them. This lets them cross the issue off their to-do list and gives you an opportunity to not only come to their rescue, but you show humility and the initiative to learn. By being a good partner to them when they ask, you show your customer you will be there when needed.

Just as you are when you're purchasing a product or service yourself, all the customer wants is:

- to be listened to and appreciated

- to have their need or promise fulfilled

When you engage with your customer, you are giving them the respect and attention they are looking for, while at the same time, showing your dignity and integrity for them and your business. These attributes will set you apart in your industry.

9) Be flexible.

It's fair to say, sometimes your strategy will go right out the window and the effects of an event will leave you with a quiet phone and an empty inbox. Don't take it personally. For every lost customer, there are ten who can't wait to have you haul for them.

Though these situations are hopefully few and far between, they do happen, and when they do, the best game plan is to adjust your sails, catch a breeze (or in our case a road), and head in a more viable direction.

The pandemic has brought chaos to the most sound of industries, leaving over 14 million people in America unemployed. It has upended many companies in the CDL trucking industry, while at the same time overburdened others.

Some trucking companies don't have enough hours in the day; consider an operator delivering groceries and food items, or another transporting medical supplies. Their industries have been moving non-stop for months, and it is likely to become overly busy again if case numbers continue to climb. For those transporting fuel or supply parts to manufacturers, it's anything but busy.

As manufacturing production dropped, so did truckers' schedules. Needs for parts and components dwindled, and as the pandemic spread and states restricted travel, so did the dynamic of the CDL industry.

A key indicator to the downturn of our industry is recognized on spot market rates and load boards. It represents close to 20% of the industry, pairing companies which need a load shipped and truckers looking for a load to fill their return or original trips.

Since March 2020, the overall number of available loads posted were up 39.1% compared to the previous year, while the increase in trucks looking for loads increased by 6.3%. As March drew to a close, however, the last week of March in particular, spot load posts dropped 38.7%, while trucks looking for loads increased to 12.7%.

The new turn? Truckers are having to hustle to find freight their trucks can move. The trucking industry wasn't part of the relief in the CARES Act (Coronavirus Aid, Relief, and Economic Security) but many companies are looking for Small Business Administration program relief for payroll and loans. Everything else is an innovative hustle for truckers who are in need of moving freight and completing runs. Though many large companies have donated funding to help keep the trucking industry afloat—Goodyear Tire & Rubber Company as well as Convoy Freight Network, for example—trucking companies are still struggling to keep their trucks running and their drivers busy.

In addition to the pandemic and the troubles it has caused, driver distraction incidents have almost doubled since this time in 2019. It could be related to a lower perceived need to focus due to the decrease in traffic on the road, or drivers under mounting stress from income decreases or health issues. Whatever the cause, the trucking industry is, once again, having to jump unseen hurdles and overcome building grief.

When considering, however, the smaller trucking business, who has 2 to 3 trucks to run and 10 to 20 customers to service, how does this scenario play out for them? No data was found, as these businesses are usually solely owned, and would most likely have to apply for any help through the Small Business Administration as did their larger counterparts. But when a small business misses 5 loads and 10 billing tickets, it is a devastating blow. Most often they can't get a piece of the available action either, due to the network of larger companies and alliances shared from within.

You, However, Are Different

With all of these facts and details affecting the small business operator, though, there is hope in the belief we will survive. Make no mistake, we will struggle and have our own share of faulty records or sick drivers. But one thing is clear. We are a feisty lot, and when one thing doesn't work, we back up and try another route.

You as a new or established business owner, will also learn how to do this, if you haven't figured it out already. Because you have seen choosing a niche can change, even in the slightest way, to create a new client base, you can evaluate new possibilities for your business and provide service to new clientele. By having the ability to create opportunities and the knowledge to adjust for changes, you will come out as a winner, banged up a bit, maybe, but never beaten.

With the knowledge this book provides, you will not only be able to change course and adjust to the new options if necessary, you will create new methods to attract the attention of your desired customers, with just the right offer at just the right time.

Remember, all your client wants is to be listened to and have their needs met; you do this for them, and you will have a loyal client for life. There are more ways to create a marketing campaign than there are stars in the sky; start small, think big, know the strategy inside and out, and expand to other ideas which link to your foundational strategy to grow your brand and your client base.

Using proven methods in the beginning can give you ideas on how to adapt the basics to your specific needs. In the next chapter you will learn how to map out your strategy in a meaningful and progressive manner.

CHAPTER THREE

Covering All the Bases

Remember when we said knowing your business objectives inside and out will give you a strong foundation on which to build your business? Well, here is where that comes into play. You know your direction, now you get to choose the tools to build your path to success.

Within marketing or advertising, you have an incredible number of avenues you can take to get your company recognized. Certain methods can utilize specific products—services may be presented better in one light than in another—and some techniques just make it easier to achieve higher sales than others.

To learn the complete strategies of marketing and the subtleties of doing one tactic and then another, people have attained degrees, written manuscripts, conducted statistical analysis, and tried many other noteworthy methods of acquiring knowledge and mastering skills. This path takes time, energy, and money, few endeavors any of us want to commit to.

Truth be told, all you have to do is know what you want your company to excel in, create this image when marketing and branding your business, and drill down to discover who your target audience is.

That's it.

Everything else is just choice and application.

Choose the result you want, work your way backward to the beginning, and see what path will get you to the goals you want to reach. By starting your marketing thought process with these simple ideas, you can get the answers you are looking for. Most business owners need multiple campaigns to figure out this simple process!

Traditional Advertising

Television ads, both local and national, cable, internet, and digital - Production of television ads can run from thousands to millions of dollars. Sometimes, if you can specifically target your idea audience on TV, then the money spent to run the ad may be worth it. If you only want a local reach, say for delivering business packages to a neighborhood pharmacy, you can purchase 'ad packages' which target a specific area. Production for your ad (or video) should also be prudent, as spending a lot of money on a commercial can easily happen when things don't go smoothly and resources have to be tapped to make it all work. Schedules put together to 'run' your ads can be expensive also, so a brief budget analysis might be a good idea to determine before you start taking videos of your crew in action.

Radio ads, broadcast and Internet - Producing a radio spot by yourself can be very economical, especially if you believe you'll be using this kind of marketing for a longer period of time, such as using audio podcasts for example. Investing in recording equipment and software can be pricey, but good devices which will serve you well can be set up for about the same price as a first run campaign. You can also use your audio recordings on other media, such as Instagram or Facebook. Many radio stations also have recording studios available to use if you want top-notch recordings for a nominal price. Talent can also be hired for production of your ads too.

Advertising on vehicles, cars, buses, etc. – With the innovation of 'wrapping,' vehicle advertising has become quite a lucrative business. For a price, you can get your message put on a vehicle which will be on the road for a designated amount of time. Buses are another alternative, and use plastic poster boards for their advertising, which has proven to be a good choice, offering many great options for print production. You will usually be locked into a longer period of time for your ad, so be strategic. Don't choose a specific promotion which you'll have to honor for longer than you can either afford or want to offer.

Industry-specific periodicals (online and hard copy) ad, article, op-ed - Targeting a specific audience can sometimes be frustrating. While advertising in a periodical or newspaper most often will be broad, it can give you some nuggets of good contact if your potential customer is tied into the same focus as your business, such as transporting thoroughbred horses. Look at the description of the publication on its website and see if it aligns with your intent.

Writing articles, guest blogs, and opinion editorials for magazines and/or popular blogs can also bring you notoriety and get your business' name out into view. If you do write, make sure your article is of interest and is written well. Make sure the grammar is proper and spelling has been checked, maybe with Google Drive or Grammarly. Considering these are free options, the advantages are endless. You could also put the same article on your LinkedIn Profile, a Facebook page for your business, and a blog post on your website. By linking the keywords and your business, the search engines will recognize your article and give it a higher preference ranking each time it's viewed, the more the better.

Purchasing a booth at trade shows, conferences - Though targeting an audience at these types of events can be fairly easy and specific, considerations need to be weighed, as these shows and conferences often draw large and diverse crowds with little else in common other than the topic at hand. Shows can be broad in attraction or very specific, such as outdoor supply retailers. You may be looking at this exact type of marketing, and if so, heed caution. This type of marketing tool is generally very expensive, not only for the space you occupy (your booth), but also the man-hours spent in planning the event, transportation and housing for hosts and booth, and additional fees tied into display and advertising of your booth (sometimes union fees, electrical needs, optional advertising packages, and set up/take down costs).

The most successful trade show exhibits are usually large companies who can dominate the trade show floor, or at least compete in it. The smaller participants most often are lost in the large crowds.

As an attendee, however, you can gleen quite a bit of information about an industry and its influences at these types of shows, and your competitors.

UPDATE: As of March 2020, most trade shows have been indefinitely postponed due to the COVID-19 pandemic. Check on industry websites and reviews for current standings and dates. If you are thinking of this niche for your company, do your homework. It's believed this industry will return, but what it will look like after the pandemic is anyone's guess.

Outdoor advertising (billboards, sporting event sponsorship, building wraps, etc.) - The sponsorships for sporting events is a very broad audience and wouldn't be prudent for many businesses. The same can be said for billboards, although if you are strictly working in local transport or logistics this could serve you well. They are a bit on the expensive side and usually run a month at a time. Again, weigh the benefits and judge accordingly for length of exposure.

Media blitz (sponsorship of a business promo, sport team, charity event, etc.) - Having an event at your place of business with a radio sponsorship broadcasting can be costly, but if executed properly, it can serve you well for quite some time, as people can have a delayed response. Usually, it's conducted as an Open House, but can be advertised with any promotion you believe may work. A word of caution: most often, media blitzes take some time to make up for their initial costs. You'll pay upfront for the radio or channel televised, which often includes a 'personality' talent fee, refreshments for everyone involved, including your team who's supporting the media, and any promotions you feel necessary for its success.

Online Advertising

Business website – As time passes, having an active and informative website is becoming as necessary as having a name. You can get business from generic searches (this is called organic response), possible engagement when the keywords you use on your website puts your name at the top of a search page, and business when a past client wants to use your services again, but can't spell your name right. All this and more is tied to having a website. More than 3.8 million searches per minute are handled by Google alone (January 2020), and to miss out on this chunk of business is like giving your competitor the password to your bank account.

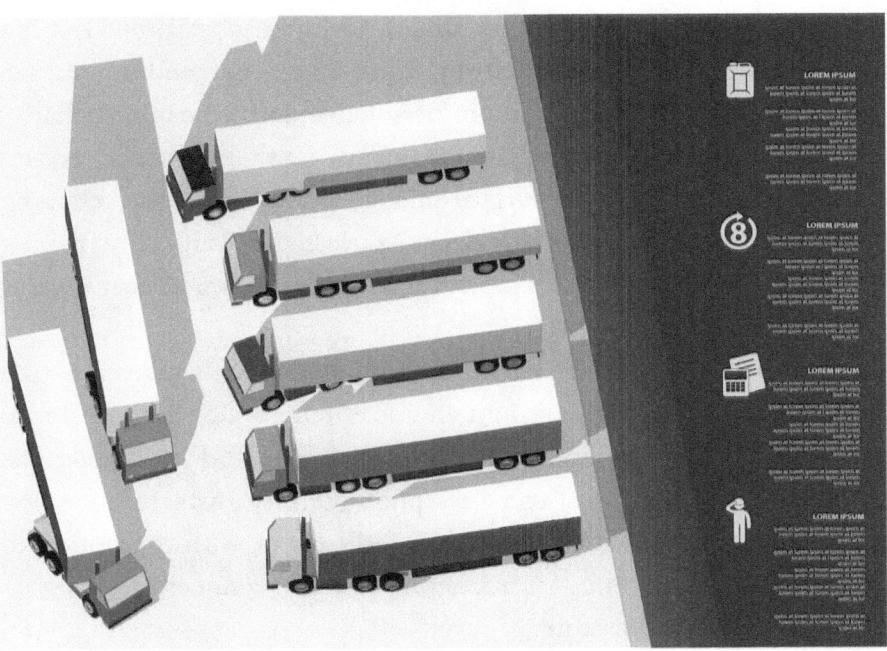

Company blog and posts - Keep your customers updated on changes and improvements, offer them discounts or bonuses with promotions during slow times, or just have a place where drivers can share. When you connect yourself and your company image to others on a more intimate basis than a handshake, an invoice, and a check, you begin to develop relationships which can grow and thrive; it's what businesses in these device-driven times thrive on.

You can also develop a following, which looks for your regular posts and is eager to support your endeavors and challenges. Consider this the replacement of a lunch and a handshake. Most days in our busy lives we don't have time to connect personally, but by sharing industry information and support, you can build networks which are stronger and have more people involved than you ever imagined. And this, in turn, brings strength and continuity to your company today and in the future.

Industry-specific blog (opinion articles, thoughts) - By writing industry-specific news articles, overcoming a common obstacle or sharing an experience you've had which you think others may find interesting, you will make your company more 'personable' and more approachable. People see you as a person when you share yourself and your ideas, and this is one of the most important things in developing and retaining client relations. In an age where devices govern our availability, making any part of those experiences more human will win over almost anyone.

Social media accounts (like a mini-website, Pinterest, Instagram, etc.) - Many apps can create an account and post items which are relevant to the creator's directives, both stagnant (a picture or PDF) and moveable (a video or phone clip). If you are a photographer, Instagram lets you post as many of your own images as you care to, with the option to 'promote' certain pictures for marketing or social connecting purposes. Pinterest is much the same.

If you choose to create a presence in any of these social media apps, read up on the basics at the website home page so you understand their rules and guidelines. If you stray from these social media's preferences, their internal algorithms will dismiss your account and postings, and it won't matter how often you log on and post content. If you are breaking the rules from the start, you will be at the bottom of the scrolling vacuum.

Most often, YouTube has incredible information in an easy-to-understand format for posting and promoting on these sites. There are also countless offers for software programs to help you navigate. You may want to save these channels for later, when you feel comfortable with your online brand and your website is running smooth.

Social media ads (Facebook, YouTube, Google, LinkedIn, etc.), can be an automated ad, video, standing link, or giveaway via email address – Once you become familiar with online sites such as Facebook, Google, and LinkedIn, you'll begin to notice the scrolling offers on the side and at the top of the pages you search. The way these recurring ads appear are devised through the now famous process of applying 'cookies,' small 'markers' which remember what you've done in the past, so they can recall and expose you to it again in the future. These can benefit an advertiser, but they can also send your paid-in-advance marketing plan into the dark reaches of cyber no-man's-land, so make sure you have your keywords and key phrases in place to 'land' on the site's appropriate page(s).

When you understand what a site offers as an advertising vehicle, you can make sure your ad abides by the 'cookies' rules and doesn't get tossed aside. You'll also need to keep an eye on your ads to make sure this doesn't happen. No one will notify you if your ads aren't making it to viewing pages. One last note: determine a budget and stick to it. Don't fall for the 'one more week' ad campaign. If it's not bringing you the numbers you are looking for, pull it, rework it, and post again for another round for viewing.

Affiliate marketing promotions (sales from a 'partner' who leads the customer to you) - This can be a very lucrative way to not only connect with industry-driven people, but you can make money and share abiding customers with other vendors you believe your clients would enjoy. It works like this: you both agree to promote a particular product or service, one of which is the originator of the item and finalizes the sale, and the other is the 'affiliate' who promotes the item to their client list and receives a percentage of any sale. It can also be a great way to share clients if you have businesses which support each other, say a vendor and a shipper combine a promotion to offer to both their client lists and split profits. Some also call these 'joint ventures.'

Webinars selling programs or group offers - If you feel comfortable in front of a camera, maybe you would like to share a particular favorite ride you do often, or want to discuss a topic of interest to several people you sell services to. Maybe you can show how to install a sound system in the cab, how to keep refrigerators and freezers performing at optimal levels (in static locations or as trailers), or how to perform specific services on your truck/trailer.

Article publication promotions (opinion article on an industry website) - If you wanted to share your particular experience with a vendor or business you like, writing an article or posting an opinion piece on their website is also a great way to get your name out and tie your business with another you admire. Sometimes you can do this openly, other companies request you have permission before posting information. Industry websites can be incredibly resourceful and offer clients and customers from places you had no idea how to reach. There are many clubs set up around small businesses and entrepreneurs, which also offer guidance and conversation between colleagues. Volunteer an article or two, and pretty soon you will get referrals from people who will like what you have to say.

PPC (pay per click) you only pay for 'clicks' of interests for an ad or promotion - As mentioned before, PPC can be beneficial if you want people to go to a specific page or place on your website. If you are promoting a special or want to share something specific, this is a great avenue to use. Many companies swear by PPC, and others have found it to be cumbersome. Do some investigating on your own; cruise through some of your favorite retail pages. Notice the ads running on the side and see if you can spot the PPC advertisers. Common characteristics are large retailer websites who are looking to sell side space on their site, such as DIY retail stores or large investment firms. The little ads change often, and usually ask for your email first, so they can send you future promotions. A local trucking company could make a lucrative business from running PPC campaigns on a local large outlet store. If you are in a long-haul business design, however, you may want to bypass this option, unless you see a perfect way to utilize the process.

A Mix of Traditional and Online Marketing

Multimedia marketing campaigns - A well-rounded marketing strategy will get you maximum exposure while narrowing in on the avenues of advertising you feel are best for your particular customer. Having a website with a blog up and running with supportive flyers posted in coffee shops or restaurants can cover a broad range of clientele without spending too much money on your efforts.

If a billboard will support your online reach and interaction, then by all means, go ahead and see where it lands. Listen to your heart, dig around to see if your ideal client profile would likely see or interact with your ads, and judge your outcomes. If the initial campaign doesn't produce success—and most likely while you are in the beginning stages, the successes may be sparse—change **one** characteristic and try it again. After you get results from that, compare it to the original and judge your outcome. Then, change another one, and run it again.

What you are doing is called 'A/B Testing' and you are comparing the first outcome to another by changing just one factor each time. It can also work well for engagement and comments on your blog or a particular promotion's draw of customers. When you combine the best of both traditional and online marketing, you set yourself up for recognition and success.

There is no single formula for a great advertising campaign – And even if there was a single GREAT formula, it would change tomorrow, just as your clients' needs change and the aspects of your business change; though, of course, there are some basics which can be used as good guidelines.

Being adaptable and learning to adjust quickly benefits everyone. It will prove well for your company to be able to recognize a poor choice and adjust for the better. It will show clients you are aware of current trends within your industry and adapt to the needed changes quickly, and it will look great on your financial statement—even as poor responses—when turned around quickly. It will be just a bump in the road instead of a major deficit disaster which looms longer than it should. Keep analyzing your results, adjust and tweak what you can, and move forward with expectations that what works today doesn't necessarily mean you're done with your marketing for the year.

The selection of the right approaches will depend on what you're trying to do and who you want to reach (where your customer is) – Know what's available to you and judge how each tool could affect your outcome. It's just like building a table; if you have a plan and use the right equipment and supplies, it can turn out beautiful. Choose the wrong tool or a weak piece of material, and the whole thing can fall in on itself. There are many options to choose from.

A combined approach employing the best of each – Depending on the direction you want your brand to take and the targeted audience you are after, having a varied plan will serve you and your ideal customer the best. Pick and choose a few foundational marketing approaches, such as an updated website design with committed blog posts, an Instagram journal of your travels, and a thank-you card sent to all new customers. Master these tools first and get to know them well, then change up a couple of things, add some new ideas to the journal or remove something which is cumbersome or hasn't received any response, and launch again. Try a promotion, change the colors on the website, word some key elements differently, each separate, and each monitored. You'll be a pro at marketing in no time, and have a dependable and stable business foundation to build your growth.

Innovative Marketing Approaches

At this point, you may be feeling a bit overwhelmed and that you may not have the skills or time to design a marketing campaign, nor the money to pay someone else to do it.

Rest assured, there are as many ways to get your company in the online sector of your niche as there are strategies to play poker. The importance of having a website, online blog, and an online journal are immense, but going online with these tools is as easy as watching a YouTube video. There are many common questions we all have when designing a website, putting together a video, or promoting your business on Facebook.

Writing effectively, for instance, comes with practice and mastering this skill will improve over time, whether it's writing an article for your blog or stating your mission statement. When you see something you like, notice the way the words are used and how they are set up to catch your attention. How did it catch your attention and can you incorporate a few items to initiate the same results for your marketing?

Noticing the things which get you in the mind frame of purchasing is the answer to developing your ideal marketing strategy. Before too long, you will master these skills and propel your company into the profits column. If you are doubting your ability to dissect another company's marketing strategy, fear not; the basics of assembling your marketing strategy and learning the secrets which will make the process easy will be shared with you in Step 1.

I feel intimidated by designing my own website, how can I write an ad?

It can't be stressed enough how important it is to have an online presence in the CDL business world today. Most of us connect with a handheld device, and when someone is in need of help, it's the first thing we reach for. It's one of the choices that your potential client reaches for when in need is crucial. If you have the answers to the problem, you are just a touch of a button away to have a customer call and get details. Make sure when you launch that your site looks good on all device faces, not just a computer.

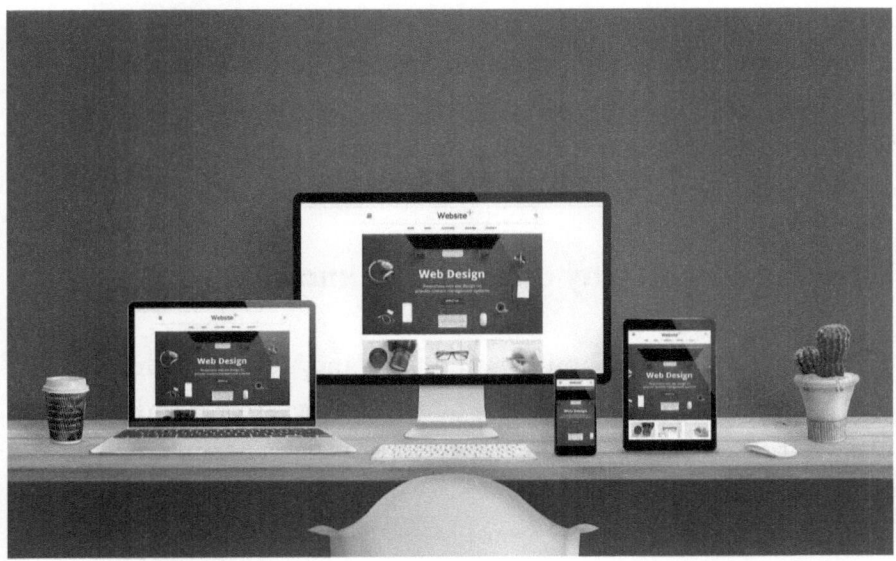

Your website is not only a 'phone listing' of sorts for your potential clients, but it also acts as a bulletin board, an online store, an update notifier, and, most importantly, a connection to your established and potential customers. When used to even a fraction of its potential, a good website will give you a thousand times back in advantages and resolve what will possibly cost in time and effort spent initially to design and launch.

If you are stopped in your tracks at this point, get someone to put a site together for you. Don't let your own insecurities stop you from 'opening shop.' If nothing more, just get a landing page (WIX is easy to use and free) with your company name, a brief description of what you offer (hopefully a promotion, keep it small but descriptive so you'll know when someone has seen it and contacts you), contact information, and a place for them to leave a message (which will drop into your email box).

Even these simple actions will get you out there and online, and build your confidence. From there, you will be surprised at how easy it is to expand into more depth and opportunities to show off your business. Here are a few terms which you may or may not be familiar with, and where they will fit into your marketing strategy.

What is SEO and why do I need to know it?

SEO, or search engine optimization, is a fancy term for what Google or any other search engine does when it lists websites in order of popularity; it takes the words you enter into the search bar and delivers the most relevant answers, or the ones with the word(s) used the most or in the same order as your search.

The more people click on a site (or pay money to have it listed first), the higher it is listed on the results of a 'search' (when you type in a subject you want more information on or to connect to). The search engine uses 'keywords' or 'key phrases' to find what you are looking for and gives you the most relevant results by using integrated algorithms. If you are a CDL operator who hauls flowers for florists, you would want to put the keywords *flowers, florists, fresh, refrigerated, overnight delivery*, etc., into the descriptions of your pages, website, and offers. By having those in specific places on your site (such as in the headings and body text), you will catch the attention of Google, Bing, etc., and they will list your site in the results of potential clients looking for a way to get their roses to the coast.

What are the advantages of having a social media presence?

Having your company's name and identity on social media platforms such as Facebook, Instagram, and Pinterest can generate interest without you even being there. And it can be free.

Let's say you have a Facebook page for Trucker XYZ. Before you begin a trip you write a little note about what will make this trip special "Heading to St. Louis today and while I was mapping the trip, I noticed there is a Hoedown Roundup in Kansas City. Here's to all the cowboys riding those broncos!" with maybe a picture of the poster, a county fair pic, or maybe a cowboy with his horse.

Simple.

Easy.

When you get experienced enough, you'll be able to link this post to your other social media pages and create 'likes' and 'looks,' maybe even some favorites and followers who find things in common with your post.

The main point here is that you are getting your company name out there. When someone 'follows' you, it kicks back to others who follow them, and they check out your page. At some point, your post can connect to a potential customer who may need you in the future, so they save your link on their list or begin to follow your posted content.

This is the power of social media, and why you not only hear so much about it, but also need to get involved with it as soon as you feel comfortable, preferably right after you launch your website!

Is listing my business in a 'niche' industry directory profitable?

Directories have been in marketing since the concept was born, and they will always have a presence in a marketing campaign. Some industry directories are more prevalent than others, depending on the personality of the industry, but for the most part, if a directory has been publishing its services for more than 5 years, it is probably still a very viable tool for the niche. Because they are delivered as an electronic file now, it is easier than ever to use them in cold contact campaigns too.

There are many ways to use a directory, anything from announcing a new promotion or delivery location to surveying potential and established client opinions. Your creativity can play a huge part when using directories, especially if you have invested quite a large portion of your budget into it. But yes, many of them can be quite expensive depending on your niche and the number of contacts you are buying.

Should I be advertising on Yelp, Google My Business, Bing Places, Foursquare, and other local online business directories?

Local citations, an SEO result which uses locations as a key factor in pulling results, have now taken searching for nearby attractions by storm. With more and more people using their GPS and navigation apps to find the nearest malt shop or how many miles it is to Winnimuka, local citations are gaining incredible weight with potential clients and customers. By having your company listed in these, particularly the ones which are more specific to CDL operations, you could be the #1 listing if someone needs to get items delivered across town or across the nation. An added advantage, if you retain a local client, it gives you advantages of keeping in touch with them on a more intimate basis, such as discussing local sports or a favorite restaurant. By having local commonalities with your customer, you can engage in ways you aren't able to with customers in other cities. It's just one more avenue to 'share' while developing your network relations with your clients.

What are PPC promotions and how would they benefit my company?

PPC is an abbreviation for pay-per-click, as we've mentioned, and is quite a simple process. If you find a website you feel your audience would connect with often, you may want to advertise on the site to grab the attention of potential customers. Many sites who draw large numbers of viewers offer PPC ads, and will sell you a rotating ad space for a very reasonable price. You are only charged for each time someone 'clicks' on your ad to view more information, which is most often linked to a landing page or promotion offered in the ad.

Clicks can run from pennies per click to dollars per click. Generally, your ad needs to benefit the host site in some way also, either by being relevant to their product, service, or subject matter, or relates to their viewers in a fairly direct way. It is an attractive way of advertising without spending a lot on your promotion. By doing your homework with analytical numbers and seeing where your clicks are coming from, you can drill down on your audience fairly quickly, and it makes it a great tool to narrow the personality of your ideal client.

I hear the term 'content marketing' often; what is it and why is it important?

Content marketing is a form of marketing which uses integral methods—such as blogging, uploading videos, or making social media posts—to promote, publish, and distribute messaging to specific audiences. By using several different media tools, a message using the same wording in all marketing methods can be marketed to similar or different audiences to produce a blanket effect of a focused advertising concept.

When we use one idea and promote it in several different ways, we create a multiple tool effect to distribute a promotion throughout a larger group. A promotion will reach many people with the same message, despite them receiving the message through one particular marketing tool or another. Your business image is focused in one direction, so you don't sell multiple ideas to overlapping audiences.

The more cohesive of a campaign you have, the better the chances are of its success.

Content marketing has become a popular concept, and was originally driven into development due to the software advantages of analysis programs. Any analysis is redundant if it doesn't compare the same concept between subjects, so campaigns began a more singular focus and created the overall concept of content marketing. A wonderful side note: the more you use it, the more it solidifies your company's marketing brand.

I keep on seeing more and more YouTube and video ads online; is this a viable means of advertising?

Business owners, publishers, and online course distributors are all moving into video promotions as their number one sales promotion to use. Even retail stores and shops are developing new ways of bringing their products to your online device via video. From demonstrations on how to decorate cupcakes to showing the steps of installing a carburetor, businesses are discovering the easy, affordable, and readily accepted form of video for their marketing campaign.

This doesn't mean you personally have to get in front of your phone and video your discount or trailer loading policies. What you can do, however, is use a video to grab the attention of a possible viewer by panning a horizon of one of your hauls and dropping in a few lines of promotion for a PPC ad, showing how to clear foggy lenses on the road, or your latest opinion of a mapping app. Whatever you want to create conversations on, you can do a video to begin the dialogue.

Depending on how serious you want to be with your filming skills, you can use your phone for an off-the-cuff ad or spend thousands of dollars for a professional grade production. Whatever your choice, there's an acceptable, good process to use, and just about anything is useful when you post it in an ad.

One rule of the marketing world which goes without any argument: your audio needs to be great. Even if the picture is too light or the words can't be read well over a background, if the audio is good, people will move along with your message and not be distracted by the lesser quality of another portion.

But if the audio is poor, you will lose their attention immediately, and in this age of point and click, you'll be dismissed without even a second thought or glance. Invest in a good recording of the audio, don't sound like you're in a barrel, and you'll be set for the video portion of your marketing campaign.

As we move forward in putting your effective and easily assembled marketing strategy together, we'll focus on the 3-Step System of Building Your Business.

In Step 1, specifics will be discussed to determine your audience in all the aspects of your business plan, from identifying your loyal customers to finding the right drivers for you and your company. You'll key into the workings of your specific marketed customers, figuring out what their problems are, the problems they need solved, and how to remedy their troubles with your solutions. You'll also learn how to uncover the clients your competition has been overlooking, making you the star for initiating a connection, helping them solve their problems, such as increasing their client satisfaction or profit margin.

Step 2 will show you how to attain and keep your best customers, without wasting time with clients who will drain your energy and give you zeros in your profit margin. Budgets, costs of marketing, tips for advantages to your specific needs, and loyalty will give you an edge for attracting great clients and keeping them enthusiastic about working with you and, in a roundabout way, for you.

As briefly talked about earlier, Step 3 begins the process, showing you the steps to take in order to build your customized marketing strategy. Earlier subjects which we discussed will come to life as you gain knowledge in terminology, understanding concepts, and how they intermingle to deliver interested inquiries to you with each marketing campaign you launch. You'll learn tools to make your life easier and what tactics will work better than others in order to give you the advantage over your competition and to get the attention of your potential clients, solve their problems with special offers, and keep them for life with incentive building advantages and attention.

The best way to launch a successful marketing strategy begins with knowing your own business personality and goals, as well as knowing who your target potential customers are. The only difference between a profitable brand and an unprofitable brand is cohesiveness, keeping your company image in place throughout your business campaign; identity and recognition are the key elements.

In the next chapter you will begin taking action steps and assembling your rock-solid game plan.

CHAPTER FOUR

Building Your CDL Brand Step One - Know Yourself, Know Your Audience

By beginning the process with solid plans and goals, you will become a successful company and attain profits and growth much faster. You will be clear on your views of how to better your company as well as have the ability to see what isn't working currently.

Now that you have decided on what your ideal business strategy will be, it's time to begin putting your ideas on paper and hold yourself accountable to your ideas and plans.

What kind of business will you be?

A sole proprietorship?

A partnership?

A Limited Liability Company (LLC)?

A corporation?

Having a clear understanding of what each of these offers, the benefits and weaknesses of each, and where you feel you'll fit in the best, is an important decision and should be made with as much knowledge and clarity as is possible to have. A brief discussion of each follows.

If, however, after reading this you feel you don't have all the answers, do more reading. Talk to other operators or owners who run their business the way you would like to. Ask why they chose the path they did, then evaluate your options. It is always a good idea to speak with legal counsel also to make sure you are interpreting state regulations, federal mandates, and business structures in the correct manner. Misinterpretation can cost you your business—and your home and assets—down the road if made incorrectly in the beginning!

Sole Proprietorships

In this business profile, it is up to you and you alone. The Internal Revenue Service (IRS) sees a sole proprietorship as a default type of company, and will automatically label your business as such if it's not stated otherwise in legal documents and licenses, such as registering in your state as a business.

As a sole proprietorship, it is easier to keep costs low, as you have the control of spending and costs, which also simplifies record keeping. If you plan on building your company with multiple trucks and drivers. However, the greater possibility of accidents increases, as well as your liability, and therefore this can affect your personal assets substantially.

An Important Note - If you don't separate out your personal assets from your business assets, they are all seen as the same thing by the state and legal system. If, for example, you default on a loan or lose your truck without replacement from insurance, your home could be repossessed to repay financial debt or loans. If you have other truckers driving for you, this liability increases also, exposing you to higher possibilities of damage and recourse.

For these reasons, maybe being a sole proprietorship as a trucker isn't the best choice for a business structure. The risks for accidents and misuse is high for trucking companies, and these risks are—most of the time—out of your control.

Independent Contractors (vs. Employees in the Trucking Industry)

Many truck drivers fall into this category. They have their own truck, but work for another person to provide a service. They are not employees of the company, however, and govern their own income tax reporting and maintenance of equipment on their own. They are not hired as part of a company fleet, but can drive for companies who have them.

Because the person or company the independent contractor is working for doesn't take income tax out of their paycheck, they receive a 1099 form for income tax reporting purposes, and can also claim expenses and other costs as part of their 'business,' such as declaring loss of value in equipment and trucks. It is a good idea to anticipate the tax requirements and make quarterly estimated payments toward the annual income tax.

An independent contractor can operate as a partnership, LLC, or corporation, though this practice isn't common.

An employee of a trucking company receives a W2 and would have tax money taken out of each paycheck to cover income tax requirements.

Partnerships

Within the structure of a partnership, both parties share ownership of the business. Both have invested in the business and both are involved in its structure and operations. From this point forward, however, duties and responsibilities can be divided separately or combined.

Value for this business structure comes from the security of having shared responsibilities, which can give the company a sizable advantage when starting up. More resources are available, and more talent can be offered, as well as money.

But the losses also are shared, and as a partnership, both parties involved are still liable for any accidents, errors, losses, and damages. You and your partner are not separate from the business and if unforeseen events cause outside parties to file lawsuits against the business, both of you will be named. And if your company can't weather the damage, your assets may be vulnerable, including homes, financial accounts, and any other material items of value.

Even if you aren't the only person who may be held responsible for unfortunate occurrences, the risks are still evident and you won't be protected if something drastic happens.

The most common types of partners are:

General Partnerships - Both entities manage the business and are involved in the direct operations of the partnership. This includes responsibility of running the company, and sharing the liability as well as its profits and debts.

Limited Partnerships - This type of business relationship has an investor, one who fronts money to the company and in return profits from the growth and revenue the business produces. They also are considered liable for debts and losses the business may experience, but have little—if any—involvement in the running and operations of the company.

Corporations

Operating your business as a corporation has some notable advantages, and separation of your personal assets from the business is one of them. *If your business fails and debts must be accounted for, you won't lose your home to pay for them.*

Based on your profits and revenue, a corporation's tax responsibility can be high or low. They can also incorporate shareholders who contribute to the company initially, and are awarded dividends as compensation when the company is profitable. Investors can also contribute to a company's well-being, while expecting growth to come back to them if they decide to sell their 'portion' of the company, or if the company is sold down the road.

Several events must happen when a corporation is established.

- They must have annual meetings to discuss and report financial statuses, with official records of who attended the meetings and what was said. These are recorded as 'minutes' and also state situations at hand and who will be involved in the handling of them and must be kept on file for the corporation.

- An organization chart must be available for public notice, showing employee titles, the upward chain of command, and basic structure of management.

- Accounting and financial statements must be documented and approved by all managing personnel and shareholders.

- Legal documents must be assembled and filed for the company.

Beyond being a 'corporation,' there are still further organizational decisions to be made. Four options of corporations are available, and they are:

C-Corporations - This structure separates the profits and are taxed separately from the owners.

S-Corporations - Most often, these corporations are not responsible for income taxes. The profits and losses are passed through the company to shareholders who report them on their own individual tax returns.

Professional Corporations - These businesses are most often assembled under a common profession or common fields of interest. Liability rests with the owners for many losses brought about by the actions of the company.

Non-Profit Corporations - These organizations are tax-exempt and function for the sole benefit of their objectives. Most often, they are businesses functioning within fields of education, charity, communities, and philanthropy.

Due to the fact that corporations are more expensive and demand more organization than the other business profiles, independent truckers and contractors don't usually set up their businesses in this manner, though if they knew the consequences of certain situations, many would investigate the possibility of doing so.

Because the shareholders carry the brunt of the burden, trucking companies need to take a second look at organizing their companies as corporations. This provides protection for the company if a lawsuit were filed and put the business' future at risk. If only for this reason alone, it may be a wise decision to opt for a corporate structure of your trucking business.

Limited Liability Company (LLC)

This structure offers a little bit of each of the sole proprietorship, partnership, and corporation. The owners—or 'members,' as they are referred to—file taxes similarly as sole proprietorships and partnerships do. They list profits and losses on their personal tax filings. An LLC can also tax themselves as a corporation, if doing so would be prudent to the business' best interest. A single member can become an LLC if they see fit. Restructuring a sole proprietorship or partnership to an LLC can also be easily done, and often is when owners become aware of the advantages.

The options available for LLCs over the rigid requirements are preferred by many CDL operators; there are no meetings to conduct, no shareholders to answer to, and no lengthy legal document filings that need to be performed.

Yet, an LLC *provides you with the protection from personal losses and damage the company may incur.* The company may take the hit for any accidents or liability of drivers and have to reorganize or file for bankruptcy, but homes can't be lost and personal accounts can't be drained due to mishaps and damage.

Considering the new advances in transportation and vehicle self-drivers, the transport industry is most likely up for some changes in the future. When you consider all the trucks on the road and all the freight which needs to be moved, there will always be a place for drivers, yet industry moves on and changes are inevitable for our industry.

The description may change a bit and the way we 'drive' vehicles on the road could alter, but all in all, the trucking industry is still a safe and prosperous business to be involved in. Technology will offer us all some incredible discoveries and choices in the coming decades. Your choice to be a part of this ever-changing and growing industry is a wise one, provided you take precautions and make knowledgeable decisions.

As for choosing an option for the type of business you are going to start, you may want to ask yourself this:

> *'If I were to have a damaging event happen, perhaps one of my drivers being involved in an accident due to negligent driving (either eating or texting while driving), and I was sued for more money than the sum total of all my trucks,*

equipment, and business assets, would I want to risk losing my property and personal assets to cover the suit?'

Answering this question may prove to be different between owners, depending on what state you operate out of and what your particular situation is. The structure should be to your company's benefit for success and for loss, and judging the factors is up to you as the business owner. Weigh your options, discuss options with professionals and family members, and set it up in the best way possible.

However, the future plays out, either entrusting your investments to drivers or depending on robotic technology to carry you through, striving for a profitable and growing business is what every owner/operator hopes for. Guarantee your success by studying the options and making the business decisions for you and your company.

Developing a Business Plan and Executive Summary

Your Mission Statement

By committing to a Mission Statement, you will have a reference for your own intentions and future business decisions. It will simplify your idea and brand, while giving you the roots of what you want your business to be and develop into. It doesn't have to be long and it can change as your business grows. We've mention and explain more about how to write your life's purpose and your mission and vision statement for your business in the book CDL Minded Entrepreneur, but for now, while you are beginning down the road to building your successful company, give yourself some foundational reference and compose a meaningful and sustainable mission statement.

- Keep it simple; one to two sentences is best

- Aim for under 20 words, 15 is better

- No fluff or fancy wording, be direct and precise

SAMPLE: *XYZ Company is committed to delivering products safely and efficiently across the Western Region of America.*

It's a good idea to keep your Mission Statement in sight, maybe as a sign on your desk or a sticker in your cab. Look at it often, and think about how you are accomplishing it day by day. Giving yourself a sense of accomplishment and pride is important, especially if you are a sole proprietor. You need to acknowledge your integrity and what you're doing it for as much as possible; no one else will be your cheerleader! And as you grow, you can also see how far you've come. Ideas are simple in the beginning, but as you succeed and grow and the complications of running your business become complicated, you'll value the simplicity of your mission statement and appreciate its directness and honesty.

What will be your service definition and what will you provide?

By examining a sample company, it's easy to see how your own will be similar as well as how you want to make it different.

> *Company XYZ sees an opportunity to offer better transportation options intrastate to farmers in the Midwest. Due to rural locations, rising fuel costs, and unreliable delivery dates, and LTL (less than truckload) shipments, XYZ believes it will be able to offer scheduled, combined pick-ups from regional areas of smaller farmers, developing a 'co-op' of delivery clients, and deliver the specific crops to nearby farmers markets and local stores for more reliable deliveries. By combining farmers' pick-ups and deliveries, XYZ will also be able to cut down on unnecessary trips, offering better prices to the farmers. The more the business plan sees success, the more areas XYZ will be able to offer their services too and build a reliable and cost-effective business. Farmers will also be offered incentives when they 'bring on' other farmers to join the delivery service. XYZ will focus on farm produce and products initially, but wants to eventually offer delivery services for grain, large crop harvests (such as corn and alfalfa), and perhaps dairy (consider growth and a 5 and 10-year plan).*

Have you thought of any additions you want to add to your business plan?

Do you have any ideas you are giving second thoughts to, perhaps thinking it may be too much work, too hard to find customers, or worry you're offering services to clients who may not even exist?

Examine a few companies you admire. Take note of their customer approach, comparing their image and marketing message as well as their size, growth, and what it must have taken to get them there.

By examining model companies and businesses, you will get a good idea of what you want to do and how you want to do it, as well as the negative things you definitely don't want to do in your business!

Put pen to paper.

Begin to write down your decisions now, and compare some aspects as you examine who you want to be as a business, who you believe your customers will be, how you think you will succeed in your industry, and what it will take to get your goals achieved.

Start with three columns, titled:

Current Views   **Possible Changes**   **New Ideas**

Answer the following questions in your chart. Keep it brief, but thorough. If you find you need more columns, add a 'Notes' column for each question to think about after you've completed this section.

What specific needs will your company require?

- Specific freight equipment needed, particularly for different types of freight

- Truckload (TL) or less than truckload (LTL) hauling

- Interstate or intrastate hauling

- Long haul, over the road, or specific geographic regions

Are you a one-person show, or will you have a team?

- Will you be the only driver with one truck, and have an owner/operator company?

- Will you be hiring other drivers, immediately or soon after you build revenue?

- What will be needed in addition to drivers?

- Back-office support

- Dispatch services

Before you open for business, what will you need?

If your company will be running its own truck(s), you will either need to purchase your fleet or have them financed. You'll need to find an equipment financing company to support your needs as well as insurance, an electronic logging device (ELD, required for insurance coverage), and drug and alcohol testing provider (also required for insurance). You will need to be compliant with the Federal Motor Carrier Safety Administration (FMCSA), and could possibly need help in seeing how to become compliant. In addition, you may want to use a *factoring company* or *fuel card provider*, making it easier to keep your fleet ready and available.

By doing a bit of research on these items and gathering opinions and reviews on specific price quotes and experiences, you will gain the knowledge you need in order to customize and move forward with your business plan, making sure you covered all the needed criteria and necessary logistics. If you are going to be traveling interstate, you will also want to research tolls and highway costs for interstate travel.

How will your company and its services differ from your competition?

Now that you've had time to think about your own business and how it will fit into the transportation industry you have chosen, it's time to drill down and be specific about your services.

- You've picked your region(s) for coverage

- You've chosen what types of hauling you'll focus on, and for what industries

- You've also decided on specialties which will differ you from other competition

If you haven't answered these specifics directly and know exactly how you are going to proceed with your business, then it's time to do this.

This is the 'fun' part of your business, because this is where you are the boss (which is why you began this in the first place), you choose the direction of your company (whether it will be you alone for the first few months until you get some revenue built up, or whether you will be leading a team of members and employees), and you will govern who your ideal customer is, their business, how you'll provide the best services to them, and how you will keep them loyal to you and come back to you for transportation needs time and time again.

While some of this may seem daunting and repetitive, being absolutely sure of what your company is providing and who you will be providing those services to is imperative; without these two pieces in place, all your other decisions will be 'what ifs' and you won't be able to build any kind of business on speculation and indecisiveness.

What will make your company stand out from your competitors?

What will be your unique value which sets you apart from your competition? Do you have a clean record and operate safely? Are your customers extremely satisfied with your service, and can you get testimonials from them saying so?

Building a great reputation as well as specifying your particular advantage over using another company will set you apart and draw in customers easier, while also satisfying your customers' needs to keep them engaged and satisfied.

What does your industry sector look like?

Is it growing?

Is it one which has 'seasons' of activity?

Are their locations you will focus on for heavy transportation?

Will you be focusing on full-loads or partial load transport?

By asking yourself these questions about your specific industry, you will be able to get a better picture of where you can find clients, and perhaps be able to identify a few additional customers in related niches who may benefit from using your services. You may also be able to see, with just a few changes here or there, other areas which can give you avenues for new business when times may slow down, or when seasonal changes occur.

But *thinking* you know your industry and actually digging in to find the numbers and facts to back up your opinions are the first steps to knowing how your niche behaves within your industry, its reaction to disruptions and change, and where your business will be placed within its growth patterns.

Also, see where your region is growing by researching some state revenue figures and where your sector's agriculture, industry, technologies, and entertainment areas are growing or reducing. In today's markets, don't assume anything is the same as it was 6 months ago.

As a drastic example, farmers who provided produce to solely restaurants and civic centers have been left without any customers to sell their perishables to. They are looking to almost give their products away, to not only keep their own business and workers moving forward, but in hopes the pandemic will subside and business will once again give them the level of sales they are accustomed to.

By providing a means to get their goods to other parts or customers, you may be able to solve their problem and provide viable resources for yourself, all in one contract. By brainstorming with potential clients, you may be able to produce an entire branch of delivery for your company you had no idea existed, and neither did your client!

Where are your potential customers?

Do you have preexisting customers who will use your services when you 'open' your business, or will you be starting without a client base? Having relationships with brokers and shippers may benefit your business while you build your company and services. Load boards may also be a good way to keep your truck(s) moving and money coming in while you are building your client base. There are many available; some cost a membership fee and others are free. If you offer services interstate, these may be of particular help. Remember, use them as little as possible, they are expensive and cost you revenue.

By creating and maintaining good relationships with the connections that provided you customers, you can not only provide long term connections but you can have the opportunity to create everlasting relationships with the shippers. And if the relationship goes sour between the broker and the shipper, or some other factor plays into their absence, you will have an established and reliable customer without having to regain trust. DO NOT, however, lure customers away from a broker or dispatch shipper; doing so will tarnish your reputation and leave you without clients or shipments very quickly. News travels incredibly fast when there is a rotten apple in the bushel.

What do you know about your competitors?

Is your business so specific that you won't have any competition and you have to convince your customers they need your services, or will you be among a few or many in your transportation service?

Take some time to get acquainted with the other companies who do business in your region, with your potential clients, and the transportation itself when comparing successful long-term companies, how many are in business, and where their biggest clients are coming from.

By doing some analysis on your competition, you will discover areas which they aren't providing necessary service. If they are delivering incredible numbers of hauls out-of-state, yet missing the needs of an intrastate niche, make note of that and see if you can fill the need. Just because they are bigger or have been in the business longer, that doesn't mean they will be the do-all service for their clients.

How do you picture growth and goal achievement?

Why do you want to start your own CDL trucking business? Why do you want to be your own boss? Focus on the reasons which have brought you to this place and keep them in your plans as you grow. There is no better incentive than to see your dreams become realities, and making sure you see those dreams come to life will feed more dreams and more realities, building your business and solidifying success.

What is your short-term growth plan?

The break-even point – when your revenue coming in and the expenditures going out are equal.

There is no loss, but there is no gain. By knowing what your 'break-even point' is, you will be able to better judge your costs and what you'll need to charge to keep your company running. Some businesses achieve this within the first year, others can take some time to achieve it.

You'll need to factor in your trucks' payments (if they are financed), fuel costs, etc., and move toward the 'break-even point' as quickly as possible, while still being competitive and marketable in your niche. Maintaining a steady and reliable cash flow is a necessary first step to achieving this. Then you'll determine what you need in order to support yourself as an 'employee' and add it into your short-term plan. Don't forget payroll in the equation, namely yours.

What is your long-term growth plan?

If you are beginning as a sole-proprietor and being the only driver in your company, but later want to grow and add more drivers and trucks, you will need to consider the additional costs and upkeep of adding more trucks, hiring drivers, and developing supporting finance expenses (dispatch, payroll, office maintenance).

A portion of all your profits should be going back into the company to keep cash flow steady, but if you are hoping to expand, you should also be contributing a portion of your revenue to an account which will act as a 'buffer' if you fall onto hard times or want to expand your business in the future. This fund will also become a viable means of safety for your company if you fall on a 'drought' of clients or need to cover an unexpected expense with the truck(s), cargo claim disputes, or covering ill personnel.

Financial Planning and Profits

Making a profit and what it takes to do it isn't simple and it isn't easy, but if you understand some basic principles and start with all your records and finances in one centralized place, it will only be a matter of entering figures and depositing checks.

What does it take to make a profit?

Here's the formula: Revenue minus Expenses equals Profit

$R - E = Profit$

If you predict your expenses and revenue in a systematic way, you will be able to see where your business starts, how it progresses, where growth or decline occurs, and how it happens. You will also be able to see what determinations have to happen in order for you to achieve your small-growth plan, and eventually, your long-term goals.

Income Statement Projections

This financial sheet will be a *projected or estimated* summary of your complete plan. It is made up of four integral parts. You may also need these projections if you intend on applying for financial business loans, intend to have investors, or want to apply for federal funding or grants.

Expenses - the costs it will take to run your business

Revenue - income you will receive from your customers for your services

Net Income - the amount of money which remains from your Revenue once you have deducted the Expenses

Income Statement - the summary of these figures and projections; your financial tool which lists the Revenue, Expenses, and any other particulars during a specific period of time (it can also be referred to as a Profit and Loss Statement, or P & L Statement)

To figure out your projected expenses and profits, you will either need to rely on your own past experiences (if you have driven your truck before) or do some research. You can talk to other trucking companies as a potential client and get rates. You can research your expenses, as we've talked about earlier. And you can use any other method to get answers you may be able to think of, such as speaking with others who own their own companies (you may want to make sure they are not in the niche you are going to do business in). Asking for advice is always a great way to get information.

While you are doing your research, you will come across two terms which may not be familiar to you

Variable Costs – These expenses are generally linked to the costs you will incur during a haul, such as fuel, food, maintenance, repairs, and lodging. The total of each will be different each time, even if the route is a reoccurring one. Variable costs will be a bit harder to determine, so when you are listing costs, error on the high side to begin with. It won't take long before you understand the different degrees of variance and can produce a figure closer to the actual costs.

Fixed Cost – The consistent costs of fixed amounts is much easier to determine, and rarely varies from one run to another. These include purchase payments (of your truck and/or office), insurance, and payroll if you have one. You will also divide your annual costs by 12 for a monthly figure for toll passes and license renewals, and add them to your monthly costs also.

You will also want to determine your *target rate-per-mile (RPM)*, which is an estimate of the revenue you need to earn per each mile driven. This will help you establish a baseline for figuring if a bid will bring your company a profit or a loss. *Estimate your desired monthly profits (begin with your break-even point and add 10% to 15%), then divide that number by the number of miles you will drive in a month.*

With these cost figures in place, you will be able to find your *break-even point.* This will tell you how much your trucking company needs to generate in revenue to cover all your expenses. Keep in mind, this is not what your company needs in order to be profitable; this is the bare minimum you need in order to not lose money. This amount will give you a base figure of what you will need to charge in order for your company to 'break even.' Keep in mind, this is a figure which does not include any money going to you personally, unless you have added a figure in for your own monthly payroll.

Here is an example of what your expenses may be and how to organize them; yours can be different, depending on your business profile.

Expenses (when applicable)	Costs
Origination and development	$
Insurance	$
IFTA	$
Equipment	$
Fuel	$
Monthly fees, passes, permits, subscriptions	$
Other	$

Of course, you may have more or less entries in your summary. By including all the possibilities here you will have, you will be able to put together a more decisive and precise estimate for your projections and strategy.

Your Executive Summary

By combining all the sections you've just worked on, you will now have the basis of your business's Executive Summary. This document will give you the entire picture of your new business. Its components include:

Company Description

- Company Name - the title your company will operate as

- Services Provided - state what you will be doing; *'truckload or less than truckload freight services'*

- Company Goals - list the main objective for operating your business; *'to grow from being a one operator company to having three drivers within the first year'*

- Mission Statement - drop in your Mission Statement here; *'Our business believes in putting the customer first, keeping their freight safe and secure'*

- Key Personnel and Their Job Descriptions - list you and your employees and the tasks they will be doing; *'Owner - me; Manager - Jesse Tatum; Contractors - Grant LaFey, Trevor Haines'*

- Differentiating Qualities of Services - list your redeeming qualities as a CDL operator for your customers; *'10 years of experience in providing efficient and reliable delivery, industry expertise, and affordable pricing'*

- Optionally, you can also include a vision statement, which talks about the future of your business - where you want to go, and what you're striving for

Company Strategy

- Industry Description - this includes what you'll be doing and where you'll be doing it; *'Intrastate transportation of agricultural goods within Mississippi'*

- Customer Description - this names your clients and customers; *'Farmers and growers found on load boards and produce directories'*

- Competitor Description - a brief description of who you'll be vying for customers with; *'small to midsize operators with similar knowledge of CDL operating'*

- Strategic Partners - people and businesses which will support you in your operations and growth; *'Fuel card companies, ABC Mechanics, Growers of the Northeast Delta'*

- Competitive Advantages - list the things you offer which your competition does not; *'24/7 pick-up, co-op team advantages, efficiency, and combined rate offers'*

- Applicable Regulation - a list of your regulating organization alliances; *'state transportation regulators, state business regulators, FMCSA'*

- Growth Plan - 1 to 5 years goal and growth goals: *'one driving operator, increasing to 2-3 trucks and operators within 6 months, Year 2 to offer dairy pick-up also, Year 5 to increase both lines to 5 trucks/operators'*

Financial Estimates

Discuss how you will meet financial obligations and maintain positive cash flow. By detailing the process below, you will cover all angles of your financial strategy.

- Variable Expenses: Direct - fuel

- Variable Expenses: Indirect - factoring, lodging, meals

- Total Variable Expenses: add both columns for totals

- Fixed Expenses: Direct - insurance, passes, subscriptions

- Fixed Expenses: Indirect - office rental/payments, business permits, payroll

- Total Fixed Expenses: add both columns for your totals

- Break Even Revenue Calculation: the formula follows, don't be intimidated, just take the figures from the columns above, and you'll have this figure

- Revenue - Variable Costs = the Contribution Margin

- Contribution Margin ÷ the Total Revenue = Contribution Margin Ratio

- Fixed Costs ÷ the Contribution Margin Ratio = Break-Even Revenue

As you can see, many factors determine your financial estimates, and knowing as much as you possibly can about this part of your business can only be beneficial. You can also hire an accountant to analyze your Executive Summary and determine ways you can cut costs, increase revenue, invest in products or systems which will serve your business, and guide you with needs for tax filing and payroll strategies (insurance, PTO, W2, etc.). But if you've kept up with what we've discussed here, you have constructed a firm business profile and established criteria necessary for opening up your business.

Marketing

Now that you have completed the Executive Summary, you are halfway to outlining your marketing strategy. You only have to decide on what marketing path you want to take and begin the process.

Here are the accomplishments you've made so far. You've done some hard work deciding the particulars of your business. Now for the fun stuff!

1. You have a very good idea of who your potential customers are.

2. You've done research and know where you can find your potential customers, or at least where to start.

3. You know who your competitors are, directly and indirectly.

4. You know the strengths and weaknesses of your industry and how your company fits into the industry niche.

5. You know what your own strengths are.

6. You know the profile of your own company and how you want the industry to see you.

7. You have a good idea of how your finances stand, where your money is, and how much you have to work with to promote your business.

Nailed it!

Now all you have to do is learn a few ins and outs of marketing, decide how you want to begin your strategy, and lay the groundwork for the marketing to build from.

Defining Your Target Audience

Being aware of your own direction gives you the outline of who you are looking for as potential customers and clients. If you are focused on hauling milk, you look for dairies. Simple, right?

Yes and no.

Yes, the dairies are a great place to start, but who else could benefit from your services? By expanding your boundaries and thinking outside the box, you will not only increase your client base and target audience, but you will have an upper hand on your competition.

Though milk transport is very specific, let's use another example to explore these ideas and get the creative juices flowing.

We've used the farmers' extra produce example before, let's try and see if we can stir any other possibilities for business while hauling produce.

Line up the necessities you need to transport lettuce, tomatoes, bell peppers, and green beans to the farmers market. The produce will be in sturdy boxes, and you'll be using a refrigerated trailer. Chances are, if you are picking up produce from independent farmers, you will be making several stops in rural communities before the major route to the market.

Who will you pass on the way?

Are there dairies who may have cheese or specialty products they would want to sell at the market too? What about the baker around the corner who bakes bread in exchange for eggs at the dairy? Or the lady with a new flock of hens who are producing enough eggs to feed an army? And maybe the melon farmer has too many to sell at his roadside stop; would he want to have his excess melons transported too?

How do you find out about these businesses, though?

You can look up the dairy, sure enough. And perhaps you'd see the melon farmer on the side of the road. But what about the baker? Or the lady with too many eggs? How do you find out about them?

You dig into your niche by way of *engagement*. And this is where your knowledge in social media, conversation, and upbeat involvement can make you a personality in your niche and bring you success instead of an Out of Business sign.

Remember, a strong identity of what your business offers gives you clarity in determining how to set up your business structure. By creating a Business Plan and Executive Summary, you give your business a road map of who you are, what you offer, and where you want to go.

In Step 2, we'll delve into the specifics of assembling your brand image and strategy, as well as approaching the task from your customers' point of view.

CHAPTER FIVE

Building Your CDL Brand Step Two - Incentives, Referrals, and Loyalty Programs

Before you begin to design your marketing program and take time to learn its concepts and tools, you need to understand why targeting is so important to your success. You have the basics, but there are just a few more tips which will change your game plan from good to great.

If you already have one or two great customers, focus on their needs and see how you solve them. Why do they come to you for services? Why are you their preferred choice over the company which is actually closer to their business? By answering a few questions, you can come up with key elements you'll want to exploit in your marketing campaigns and strategy.

Furthermore, wasted time is wasted effort, and it costs you money in the long run. By not being clear on who you are the best transportation service for, you will lose clients simply because they've come up with their own conclusion of what you offer. By trying to cover too many services or gather customers in an industry you are not familiar with, you will depict a lax dedication or be labeled as an imposter in the industry. You'll be doing more harm than good to your company, and the customers won't even look at your costs or details.

Honesty in business (transparency) is not only 'gold' for success, but it's the only policy towards success. Being transparent to your clients and customers is not taking credit for being the best in your sector, no matter how small, and will draw your ideal customers. These are the people who will not only call you every time without pricing out competition, but they will spread the word of how great your service is and how pleased they are to have found you. When a customer is this happy with you, they will go to the ends of the earth to celebrate your success. They are your 'champions' and can illuminate even the darkest of times.

We've talked about this many times already.

Having this business structure is exactly where you want to be as a beginning business owner in the CDL transportation business. There are other lines who will undercut your prices and there are other companies who will promise quicker delivery. But if you offer sincere integrity, great specialized service, and, above all, individualized customer care, you will bring back those customers time and time again, and they will lay your path to business success.

Now, you will find out how doing all this over-the-top customer care will come back to you in profits!

What price will you pay to find your customers?

In other words, how far will you go to uncover the secret location of your perfect clients?

Will it be the expense of time it takes you to learn how to launch a business website?

Will you spend considerable time designing your website so you can attract your ideal customer?

Will it be the money you paid for the list of potential businesses in the region that you are covering?

Or will it be thousands of dollars you expect to pay for the advertising ads you intend to post?

When you think about getting more customers and how you might go about finding them, who do you think will know the personalities of your potentials, aside from you?

Who has the knowledge of how your business performs, directly?

Who knows the care you take in loading freight, the extent you'll go to when you promise you'll deliver 'on time,' or the extra precautions insured to run a mechanically sound and maintained truck and trailer?

Who has, without a doubt, the best description of how you saved their full load shipment of fresh frozen flounder from thawing in the Arizona sun when a well-known shipping company (who won't be named) used a 30- year old refrigeration trailer, pulled from decommission, to deliver your 'high-end shipment' to a 5-star restaurant?

Exactly, *your present customers.*

Number 1 - Your Current Customers and the Cost of Customer Acquisition

The people who call you, no matter the freight, no matter the destination, because they know you will do whatever it takes to take care of their needs. And you'll do it with a smile, with a fair rate, and best of all, with their best interests at heart.

These companies, these people, your customers, are your best promoters, and usually, they are the least expensive too. Since you have shown them exactly what you do in order to deliver the best service possible, they will sing your praises and do whatever it takes to make sure you are known as the 'best in your business,' especially if you respond to their individual needs and have an engaged client relations program.

Remember, your clients are smart too, they are loyal, and their best interests are in your success. Without you being in business and surviving, they will be left in the cold without the attention and care you've shown consistently. They deserve to be shown appreciation and attention.

For you, they are also your best marketing tool.

So, with all this power of their word and praise, how can you turn their loyalty into new clients?

Show your gratitude with more than your voice

First and foremost, don't forget their loyalty. Before using their testimonials or referrals, make sure they realize how thankful you are for their words. You don't have to give them a discount on their next shipment in order for them to respect and recognize your gratitude. Although, this would be a highly appreciated service!

Build a referral program for them and use incentives to create a two-way street of growth and prosperity. This all begins with a conversation and being interested and engaged with your customers.

Making personal and unique contact with each customer is easy.

- Send a handwritten 'thank you' note after shipments, especially to new customers or for a particularly unique haul or circumstance. Receiving this in the mail will catch their attention also, and double the response and appreciation.

- You also have an easy tool at your fingertips by sending an email or post, saying thank you for their business, or commending them on a special success.

- Post a picture or a quick video on your website about an experience or how a customer made your day will also show a sense of appreciation and comradery.

These little 'gifts' stand out from the everyday experience and are treasures; your customers will remember your thoughtfulness for a very long time. These gestures will set you apart from your competition also, gaining devotion and loyalty with only a few keystrokes or stamps.

Referral programs offer something in return

How do you ask a customer for an endorsement without being pushy? It isn't as hard as it sounds and it can be done in a creative manner. By engaging your loyal customers, you are giving them the chance to become more involved with you, if they choose, and also be rewarded for their efforts with something you choose to offer. Here are some ideas to get you started.

- Offer two free tickets to the movies for posting a short comment of their recent experience with you to your Facebook page.

- Have a contest for a two-night get-away at the local bed & breakfast for the Best Karaoke Video, creating a song about your company and singing its praises.

- Combine rewards for your existing client as well as the clients they 'bring in.' The reward doesn't need to be related or expensive, but it should be considered a reward for both clients.

Here are a few 'tips' which will make your program more successful and produce happier customers.

- Be very clear, upbeat, and honest when promoting your program. Post the terms clearly and make sure there is a place for questions if they have any. State the contest in a positive manner and don't make it sound as if you are 'fishing' for compliments or recognition. Your program has a very large chance of backfiring if this happens, so have someone else read it over and make sure it is only asking for honesty in a very gracious way.

- Make it easy to sign up for. Make needed links obvious and post conditions and terms prominently. Post the contest or program on all your marketing media. Once again, making sure you are clear about the participation and terms they may have to abide by. Signing up should also be easy to understand and simple to do.

Ask for their thoughts with surveys

You can also send out customer surveys asking about their experience after a shipment is delivered or how they like the new invoicing process. This gives your customers an easy way to give you feedback. You also can pull analysis results from them which, depending on how you ask them, can give you ranking within your industry, confidence in your ability to deliver on time, or ease of using your online scheduler. You can even find out how many of your clients rate you 'excellent' or find the percentages of returning customers who would use your services again. By posting at the beginning of the survey that all responses are anonymous, your answers will be more honest and give you information which otherwise might be hard to collect.

You can also add a block which is an 'open' response, allowing your customers an opportunity to give individual feedback. You may receive critical responses, yes, but don't overlook these gems; they are opportunities for you to make a situation right by stepping forward to correct a mistake or fix a problem. You may not turn everyone's opinion around, but more often than not, taking the initiative and doing your best to make things right will create respect and, possibly, an opportunity for a second try. In the very least, you will learn of discord in your business and can fix the problem.

Take their words to the bank - referrals & testimonials

If you find yourself able to use direct quotes from your customers, use them. Be very careful that you quote their response *exactly* as they state it. Don't feel you need to build it up or correct their grammar. The beauty of quotes is the tone in which they are said, and unique nuances and intellect shows the individual personality, diversity, and sincerity of your patrons.

Use them creatively also, and always make sure you have their permission. Even if they have given their permission before, ask again if you want to re-use a comment or draw on a new one. Never assume anything when you are stating a person's comments and signing their name to it publicly.

Try these, or create your own ways of promoting, the options are endless:

- On the side of your truck, you could put a sideline under your business name, in a small cursive script, (on a removable magnetic sheet would be best); *'Best Truck Service This Side of the Mississippi' - Dalton Dairy.*

- Or you can add a quote under the subtitle on your website; *'Delivered My Goods When No One Else Would' - Beverly Handly.*

- And don't forget the brief video of George's elated smile when you pulled in with his chickens which had been 'lost' in Wichita, but your truck saw the broken down trailer and brought the cluckers 'home;' *'They helped the original broken-down truck move my chicken crates to their empty truck and finished the route- I didn't lose a single bird!' - George Hastings, Hastings Flock & Fowl.*

The more you use your referrals and testimonials, the more you will realize new opportunities where their support can be used to spread your message. Satisfied customers are like nuggets of gold; you must protect them and do everything you possibly can to keep them in your possession. It isn't an impossible task; by being honest, grateful, attentive, and sincere, you will collect priceless marketing advantages over any competitors 'deal' or 'promotion.'

Number 2 - A Website

While it seems unimaginable for you to launch a website, it can be done fairly easily, and you can do it by yourself if you do a bit of reading, have a laptop or computer, and a connection to the internet.

You will need to purchase a web host. They are the techies who play the part of gatekeeper to your website, they are in charge of keeping your website 'up' and available, they support the site when things go wrong, and they can provide extra services such as email and security walls for you, and quite often offer many other services (you may never use). According to Brad Smith, Editorial Staff at Hosting Facts.com, the Ten Best Website hosting services are, based on speed, uptime, and costs are (as of February 2020):

1. Bluehost - Best Overall

2. HostGator Cloud - Best Cheap Cloud (has a lot of information storage)

3. Hostinger - Cheapest Price

4. GreenGeeks - Best 'Green' Hosting

5. DreamHost - Pay Monthly, No Higher Renewals

6. SiteGround - Best Customer Support

7. A2 Hosting - Fastest Shared Hosting

8. WestHost - Great Uptime for the Price

9. GoDaddy Hosting - Reliable, Good Extra Features

10. Site5 - Unmetered Storage

While each has a benefit listed, don't totally rely on this to make a choice. Go to this link for the full review of each (yes, do it!) and a chart of 30 of the most popular host services and their ranking highlights.

Best Web Hosting (2020) Hosting Facts

Depending on which host you choose, you may have website design services included with the cost, or you can use free services, such as WordPress, SquareSpace or Wix. Or, click here for a recent article of the latest and greatest according to Website Builder Expert: 11 Best Free Website Builders.

Take the time to read through these sites and articles. When you finish (might take you 20 to 30 minutes, a bit longer if you want to become an expert), you'll know all about website design and building, web hosting, and how to pick the one which will be the best for your business. If you still haven't found an exact fit, do some research and read a few independent articles (not the ones which are paid-for ad listings at the top of the search pages). There, you will find the best information.

Number 3 - Become Part of the Social Media Connection

Being savvy with social media isn't just a 'trend' that's set aside for the techies and the younger generations. These days, everyone is connected to the Internet, especially since lock-downs and social distancing have become a mandate due to the pandemic. If your business isn't present online, you are failing at keeping connected, and being connected is the bloodline of your trucking operation.

In a recent survey of CDL operators, when asked what social media platform truckers prefer (TruckersNews, D. Hollis Feb. 2020), Facebook led the pack at 63% surveyed. YouTube followed at 54%, 15% preferred Instagram, and 14% liked LinkedIn the best. Surprisingly,

Twitter came in around 13%, followed by Pinterest at 11%. Here's the full article Truckers Favor Facebook, Which Turns 15 Today [2]. Can you figure out another reason why this article may be important for a business?

If you were running an ad on a social media platform for truckers, where would you get the most viewing? Yes, Facebook, according to this article. But since your target audience isn't truckers (well, probably not), then this won't be any more of a passing interest note and connection to a like-minded individual such as yourself.

But, after reading the article, you can see the power of social media, especially for you and your CDL business. If your targeted client is also consumed by their business and unavailable most of the day, unable to view your ads on social media, when they do eventually connect with these social sites it can be incredibly powerful, especially if they were thinking earlier in the day they should try a new transportation line for their products. Customers looking for quick solutions to their problems are in every crack and crevice of your niche. Never underestimate the power of social media. As you become more familiar with the 'producing' side of social media, you will understand how important having your business present online and how simple and cost-effective the resources can be.

By having an online presence, you are also providing your intended customers and clients a resourceful place to get more information than what a television ad or radio spot can offer. It spotlights your specialties, gives an in-depth account of your business philosophy, acknowledges the specifics of your particular niche, and offers personal interest articles and access if they want to get questions answered, even when they are viewing your site at 11 at night.

When you see all the benefits that having a current and interactive website offers your potential as well as established customers, you can also see how it will be the command center of your marketing campaigns, at affordable prices with a reach of thousands.

Tying your online presence with traditional advertising

There are a million and one ways which are advantageous to running a multi-level campaign for your business. That is, if you have a million and one dollars to spend, and if you have the time to sketch out and purchase all the supporting space, time, and schedules which are needed to launch such an elaborate crusade.

The simple fact is that, with a few clear ideas and a couple of sensible actions, your marketing launch stating you're *open for business* doesn't have to take any longer than a few hours, some creative ideas, and a collective plan (and maybe just a few dollars to get the ball rolling).

When you have your website up and running, you can create emails, send newsletters, create blog posts, and begin discussions on industry trends. The more clients, customers, and interests you add to your email list, the more opportunity you have to create a business and bring in added revenue. There are many tools by which you can gather email addresses for promotions and print flyers to get your name recognized.

But first, you need an image, something which will be recognizable to your customers immediately and can resonate in your industry with your business attached. You need a logo.

Design something simple, clean, usable, and recognizable. Think car vectors; they are logos, such as the Mercedes-Benz circle or the Subaru oval with the constellation. They all symbolize something specific within the company, yet are simple, identifiable, and recognizable to the outside world.

Try to not get too wrapped up in this process. But also pick something which you can live with, as you will be using this on everything, as an icon by your business name, next to your website address in the search bar, on the invoices you bill out, as well as the newsletters you connect to your audience with. It will be emblazoned on the doors of your truck and possibly on the sides of your trailer(s). Think of this logo as the 'face' of your business, with the design depicting your business' personality and image.

If you need a designer to help you come up with a few ideas, check out Freelancer or Upwork. They will be able to give you some different samples and you won't have to spend a fortune for the artwork. You can work out the terms for your contract, say maybe two edits or five designs. You know the secret though: simple and specific.

This design will be the foundation of all your marketing strategies and it will be recognizable within your industry and throughout your audience, if you use it wisely and market yourself in strategic places.

Always remember...

It's easier to keep customers happy, than trying to win them back. Make sure once you have a customer, you keep the connection fresh, relevant, interesting, and above all else, *all about them.*

When building your marketing strategy, use the same words, logos, and bylines; repetition is a good symptom of recognition.

In the next chapter you will learn easy tools to use for client engagement and retention within your focused and specific niche.

CHAPTER SIX

Building Your CDL Brand Step Three - Reach Your Clients and Grow Your Business

Use the Right Niche Channels to Grow Your Outreach

Your website is up, you have a logo in place to use throughout your marketing, and you've realized the strength of online and traditional media tools for your promotions. In this chapter, you will learn how to put these strategies into action and interactive methods of applying the best means needed to achieve your goals.

You've also seen by researching a few things here and there that you don't need a lot of money to promote your business to your niche. Knowing how to assemble your strategy using free, inexpensive, or incentive-driven services can give you the means to reach your target audience while still maintaining your budget. Being specific with your strategy will keep the promotion focused while promoting directly to your audience; identify the right channel for your promotion and you will connect with your customers in a meaningful way. Also, if this is your first website or business launch, learning for free is much better than learning at a high price.

Facts are facts; if you don't get your amazing service in front of the amazing customers who will benefit from your services, your business will go nowhere. You also know that, with the right strategy, you can send the perfect message that will resonate with your potential customers.

So which marketing methods and channels are right for you?

We've talked a lot about strategy, but how do you figure out what 'strategy' is best for your business? We'll go a bit deeper to get specific about the terms and clarify what would work best to reach your customers.

You already know what your perfect customer profile looks like. Whether it's the retail purchaser at the department store downtown or the medical supply coordinator at the hospital, you know who you can provide the best services to and why they will love your company.

You not only know where this customer lives but you know the websites they visit as well as the activities they do in their spare time. Or do you?

Do you know what websites your ideal customer visits? Do you know what activities interest them and where they might spend their time? You probably do, but chances are you may not realize it yet.

By putting together a strategy, you will get your message in front of your ideal customer without too much effort or money. If your ideal customer would have you ship racks and racks of clothes from NYC

CDL MINDED MARKETING

to Los Angeles, this person probably spends time on trending websites for clothing, maybe the most popular blog on similar items like shoes for women or affordable clothes for teens. Place an ad on like-minded sites for connection.

How do you find the sites your customers visit? Think like your customer and make a list of the keywords you think your customer would use to search for their interests.

'Latest fashions in Europe'

'Cheapest clothes for women'

'Comfortable and affordable pants for men'

'Dress displays and racks'

Whatever you think your customer might search, type it in and see where you go. You may hit a dead end, but you may also find a few niches which you hadn't thought of. Also, scroll down your search list and see what words are popular in the descriptions of the sites. Here, other tidbits of information can be found which may lead you down a profitable path...

If you type in a word in Google and then hover over the search bar, you'll get some related terms to the word you typed. There are also some sites that can give you keywords similar to your own words. Try WordStream to give you more options for keywords and phrases related to your searching. They offer free trials, but do charge for access after a certain amount of time.

Most likely, your ideal customer spends quite a bit of time online. Will your customer read the news, catch up on blogs, check email, online shop, or download games? See if you can find out where your competitors are advertising. If they are spending money, chances are they feel like they are in a successful place to spend more money to advertise. Check it out.

As you investigate the options, you will also, no doubt, come across apps which say they can save you time and money and assemble a marketing program, quick and easy for you. Some of these are great, others can be useless. Approach them with caution, and always make sure you know what they are talking about. If the site keeps on using phrases or terms you are unfamiliar with, find out what the phrases mean too, know exactly what they offer and how it works. Some sites can also be expensive and could promise you the world (such as 'you'll receive over 40,000 views in 24 hours'); be smart, be wise, and investigate with a wary eye.

CDL MINDED MARKETING

To show several methods of marketing to a specific audience, let's examine a few examples.

Scenario 1

Interstate CDL business, ABC Freight, wants to increase their customer base for coast to coast dry freight. This company has 20 trucks, and uses independent drivers when needed. For the past 2 months, business has dwindled, grounding 2 to 4 trucks each week with no business for their independent drivers, who are now moving to other companies for business. ABC Freight needs more schedules, preferably from container docks, which are fast easy business for them. They choose to run several TV advertisements in New York/New Jersey, Savannah, and Virginia for the East Coast, Los Angeles, Long Beach, and Oakland on the West Coast, and Houston and Miami for the southern ports. They will support these spots with the same promotion in the TV ads, with promotional email notices to all their existing customers, offering 10% off scheduled deliveries for the next 2 weeks. They have designed landing pages to accept the clicks posted on their emails, as well as stated phone numbers and website addresses on the TV ads. The home page on their site also has the promotion positioned in their banner at the top of their site as well as an upper half-screen 'ad,' which will load prominently on any device, computer, laptop, phone, or tablet.

TV production costs - $2,500.00

TV schedule on regional demographic specific channels - $550,000.00

Design and post of home page and new landing page - $500.00

Email promotion (writing, design, link insert, and email address sort) - $450.00

Total Promotion Costs $553,450.00

New Customers - 15

Existing Customers Scheduled - 28

If ABC Freight wanted to see the value of their advertising investments by translating it into cost per new schedule, they could send out a survey after attaining the new clients to see where they had learned about the promotion. Or, they could have had a check-box on the scheduling page or when they spoke to your scheduler to set up their haul asking where they had learned about the promotion. This would be a very sensible idea and, with ABD Freight being a large company, chances are they will have a similar analysis tool in place to see just how strong each of their promotional tools paid out.

Scenario 2

Northwest regional freight company, Joe & Jane's Flying Fish Freight, is hoping to expand into a few more states with longer hauls, building their pick-up base as well as expanding their delivery region outside their present region of Washington state. They offer guaranteed delivery of shipments in under 10 hours and believe even by extending their delivery area, they will be able to maintain their objectives. They've added two new trucks to their fleet and are hoping to bring in new customers in adjoining states. Joe & Jane's Freight has decided to do all of their promotion online, using their own blog posting on their website (they have 500 followers) and also a direct email launch. They plan on featuring a three-email series of videos, focusing on company values, driver profiles, and specialty truck innovations which set them apart from other delivery companies in the state. Throughout the videos, they will portray their value, ingenuity, sincerity, and connections to existing customers, as well as their initial business objectives and how they've grown in the past 2 years. Not everyone who follows their blog posts and who is on their email list is a customer.

Production of promo home page and landing page for scheduling online - $45.00

Production and editing of 3 videos with Joe and Jane and others - $250.00

Merge of emails for a 3-day send, 700 addresses - $25.00

Miscellaneous costs - $100.00

New customers - 5

Expansion of new customers into Oregon, deliveries to Idaho and Oregon

This campaign for Joe & Jane was extremely profitable. They gained 5 new customers, adding to their client base, and by doing so will be expanding into new regions for deliveries. With the agricultural opportunities presented by Oregon and Idaho, they are hoping to get return customers also, and will launch another promotion to the growers in these regions to make their new commitments even more advantageous.

These scenarios are both fictitious, but you can see how a marketing promotion can play out in specific situations. By combining methods and tools with a bit of ingenuity and planning, your company can profit greatly. You do need to plan, and you do need to know the tools and methods you are using to take advantage of all the options which will benefit your promotion.

Following below is a list of specific channels which can help you organize the strategy of your marketing. Discovering the many uses of how they can benefit a campaign may even trigger thoughts of your own on how to use their technique and approach.

Referral Marketing - This strategy builds from the generosity and word of mouth from your existing clients and customers, and should be used with every business, as a promotional campaign or an ongoing program.

Content Marketing - Any traditional or online marketing which educates your potential customers using specific wording for increased traffic on your website, clicks on your links, and followers who engage in your marketing.

Newsletters - These are excellent vehicles for your potential and existing email list. You can keep your readers up-to-date on a new discount offer, discuss the latest ruling on permit increase costs, or have a contest. It can be informational, promotional, an opinion, or sharing stories from the road. Use a free service, such as Canva, to make them appealing and entertaining.

Search Engine Optimization (SEO) - By using keywords and phrases, search engines draw organic traffic (people who are looking for information on terms you've included in your marketing) and list you or your publications on the results. By using these terms in your blog, you can also draw traffic to articles and ideas you have on your website.

Podcasts - You will see these offered more and more, as they are easy to produce and cost very little. Most are written as an educational lesson with an option to purchase something at the end. If you are the writer type, you could put together a 10-step program to teach drivers how to pack for a long haul or review the top 5 best travel mugs available.

Public Relations - Refers to business activity used in traditional media outlets, such as public gatherings, conferences, and events. You may sponsor a booth at an arts festival or donate to a worthy cause for a listing in their news bulletin.

Speaking Engagements - Industry conferences, trade show demonstrations, community growth events, and town halls all can be an avenue for your business awareness and presence. Keep an eye on the city and community dates for social gatherings which may benefit from your knowledge and guidance, as well as you from theirs.

Online Advertising - Includes the purchase of PPC (pay-per-click) ads, social network display ads, banner purchasing on websites, and promotional videos on YouTube.

Traditional (Offline) Advertising - Printed publications (brochures, business cards), radio ads and info interviews, TV advertising, magazine ads, and trade show booth promotions.

Email Marketing - A direct and resourceful way to reach your existing and potential customers, usually have shown some kind of interest, unless you are using a purchased email list. Campaigns can be run as automated (sending a message when they click on a link) or targeted (using your own list, for example) promotions. A tried and true strategy.

Sales Playbooks - The creation of specific actions, usually used when a lead list is involved, to move a potential customer into a purchasing customer.

Online Events - Includes online webinars, demonstrations, workshops, and education using online software; range in costs varies.

Offline Events - These are person-to-person or crowd events, and use trade shows, seminars, demonstrations, workshops, showcases, and customer appreciation events for building customer relations.

Utility Marketing - Software tools which stimulate traffic, sharing between users, and brand awareness.

Influencer Marketing - A practice used when building relationships with people in pre-established communities and gatherings; think of clubs, influential memberships, and elite social circles.

Partner Marketing - Co-marketing activities with other like-minded businesses which are launched simultaneously with another company with similar interests.

Social Media Marketing - Building engagement between people and businesses on established social network platforms, such as Facebook, LinkedIn, Pinterest, etc.

Community Building - The process of accumulating people and communities who support the same cause and join together to build growth.

As you read through this list, I'm sure you were able to focus on the methods you thought may help you design a campaign, while others definitely were not going to be of any help or advantage. That is the beauty of having a large choice of options for a specific directive outcome. These have proven valuable to someone and some industry as some point in time. The longer we promote, the longer this list will become.

The point is this: you know your company, you know what types of promotions are appealing to you and which ones you will stay clear of. Use the ones you like, expand in a couple of areas if you are curious to see how they may perform for you, and then evaluate and choose the better ones for you. In a year or two, perhaps your business will take a turn and something else will look more advantageous. There is also the proverbial growth thing; new methods and channels appear all the time. Something which sets your company on fire may not even be conceptualized yet.

When analyzing your promotion after its finish, be sure to attribute the correct channel with the correct result. The fact that you now have more customers can be due to the fact that you emailed out the availability of a refrigerated truck for hauling, but it also may be because your new driver connected with a group of haulers who were overworked and in need of some help in hauling produce.

Don't be afraid to mix it up and try new things. When you do, though, make sure you are changing just one item in your promotion, so when you evaluate its results to previous promotions, you are able to see specific differences instead of trying to guess which one of the three changes was responsible for its result.

Setting Goals and Working Optional Objectives

You may from time to time come up with a goal you want to achieve, perhaps delivering interstate or offering more options of freight contents, but you aren't quite sure how to reach the people who would be involved in this new pursuit.

When you are familiar with different channels and methods of assembling a promotion or service launch, go back to the basics. Picture your ideal customers.

- What are their characteristics?

- Where will you find them?

- Plan a strategy of reaching them with whatever means you believe will be successful.

By going back to the basics and starting with a new plan, you are thinking clearly on the focus of a new customer. You are also broadening your options for opportunity instead of reconstructing an old method with means which worked for one set of criteria, but aren't necessarily good for your new set of criteria. And, best of all, you are building your own marketing prowess, using all options, some of which may be new tools, and stretching your creativity in new ways. This is not only good for you personally, keeping you sharp and energized, but it also will keep you one step ahead of your competition.

You are the innovator, action taker, and decision maker.

You are creating new methods.

You have the advantage of using new ideas over old.

Every so often, you may get stuck on an idea, or use the same promotion too many times, resulting in poor interaction and growth. These are signs of a stagnant marketing offer. Make notes, record results, and move on. When you find a method which doesn't meet your expectations, analyze the promotion and the tools you used and see where the broken link is.

You may want to fix the link by changing just one little component, which can be as simple as a color on the landing page or a word in the header of your email letter. Whatever it is, change it and try again.

But if you feel it may be an entire revamp of the promotion, don't waste your time in procrastination or analysis. Make the change and move forward. Nothing wastes time and money more than the repetition of pondering a broken method.

As you do your research, analyze the best strategies to reach your ideal customers, launch those promotions, and search the results for most activity and best sales. Take notes and imagine the results of a change or two.

What can you do differently next time which may reach more viewers?

What engagement seems to bring more viewers to your social media page? What engagement seems to bring more viewers to your podcast? What engagement seems to bring more viewers on your website?

Would relating the blog to the promotion bring in more views and more possible customers?

Would you change anything?

And when you're ready to do it all again, take a big breath and dive right in; lather, rinse, repeat.

Don't forget...

Take a plan, run the analysis, and then outline realistically where you want to be in 6 months, 1 year, 5 years, and even 10 years into the future. A measurable vision can lead to realizing your goals down the line; keep on reinventing your channels and methods, your strategies, and your promotions. When you're done, do it all again!

In the last chapter we'll be wrapping up your plan and taking it to the next level.

CHAPTER SEVEN

Your Successful Launch

Starting a business is more than just loading up your trailer and driving into the sunset. It is a work of love, and every effort brings you closer to achieving your dream of owning a successful and thriving business. You've also realized there are a few things you'll need to learn, and probably learn again. The best part about your venture is this:

You are the boss.

You govern the direction, and

You are able to plan your own future.

When you have run a few promotions, you'll be able to govern your channels better and identify your ideal customers more easily. The more you involve yourself in the process, the more you learn, and, obviously, the better and more proficient you will become at devising and assembling successful campaigns.

Don't be discouraged if a promotion you spent a lot of time on falls flat. In all reality, prepare yourself for it. Chances are it will happen at some point and you will have to deal with defeat. More likely than not, deflating occurrences happen as you are learning how to market and launch promotions, which makes the defeat seem larger than it really is.

Here is where your budget comes in and plays a key role in your game plan.

By not paying out too much money, actually any at all, you create a bumper of sorts, cushioning the loss and easing your burden. Yes, you spent a lot of time on the promotion, and yes, your time is money.

But also flip the coin and realize what you have learned.

Chances are, you have a pretty good idea of what not to do. Ask yourself the questions we discussed and see if there is room for changing up a couple of key components. Maybe email isn't all you hoped it would be, or maybe people aren't coming to your website as much as you thought they were.

Is there a small change you can make without having to plan an entire campaign?

Of course there is.

Often, we are lured into thinking a particular marketing path will be exactly the route to take. When reality hits, usually in the form of the sound of crickets, we'd be smart to take a step back and see if we were swayed by fancy sparkles and twirling lights.

There are many programs available promising 'do all promotions' and 'sell numbers' that would make Warren Buffet buy in. Facts are facts, and no matter the promise or the pitch, these 'do all' promises are like dust in the wind.

See if you can come up with one really good idea to pull more viewers to your website.

By writing a blog about your ideal customers' biggest pains and emotional struggles, this will attract their attention so you can give them the information they need.

Start a newsletter, just a one-page email, and discuss a recent experience you had that you think will be interesting (or entertaining!) to your industry. Maybe you'd feel better about sending it to one or two of your colleagues to see if it is as industry specific as you want it to be. Afterward, email it to everyone you know. Even if they aren't truckers, they may enjoy hearing about an adventure you had, or they may even share a laugh with you.

Strike up conversations at truck stops and regular places you frequent. See if anyone else has a story or maybe would like to contribute to your website. Make sure all information goes through you first; don't ever let anyone post directly on your site, even when responding with a comment or post.

There are 'bot sites' and destructive hackers who can cause all kinds of havoc, and securing your website is just one more thing you won't have to worry about. If you choose a responsible web host, they will have options for you to choose from, which will give you control over who has access and who doesn't.

CDL MINDED MARKETING

With that said, let's review a few things you have learned reading this book:

- You have written a Mission Statement and Business Plan, along with an Executive Summary and Financial Estimates, which will not only be a welcome tool for accounting, but will be needed if you are looking for additional funding or partnerships.

- You have legally established your company and understand the necessity of properly setting boundaries between your personal assets and business liabilities to protect, not only property and assets, but also loved ones and family.

- You know and understand the business side of having a trucking business and are equipped with successful and proven strategy methods to make your company thrive.

- You know how to determine who your best customers are, how to find out where they congregate, and how to attract and retain their trust and business.

- You understand the reasons for evaluating a marketing plan and the benefits which can be found by actually doing so.

- You have either mastered or will master software apps which will make your business run smooth and soundly, even when you aren't there to monitor it.

- Most importantly, you understand the weight of having a satisfied customer, how their satisfaction can be turned into advertising for you, and how you both will benefit from engaging in a trusting and supportive relationship.

A final note on our current conditions and how this may affect our industry in the future.

None of us knows quite how long the COVID-19 pandemic effects might last or how far-reaching into the future they may go. Our industry has seen exponential growth, and, currently, many companies are setting up shop without having a clear grasp on what running a trucking company demands or what is required for it to be successful.

But one thing is clear.

You will be ahead of the crowd by using the methods stated in this book.

The pandemic crisis will be around for quite some time, either directly or indirectly with fallout and lasting circumstances. The businesses who survive and make money during this unpredictable time will be the businesses who can adapt, invent, show dependability, and create new avenues in which to run their companies and provide service to their customers. In other words, change won't keep you from working.

With the tools you have from this book, you also have the power to invent your future and create a sustainable lifestyle by comparing, analyzing, creating, testing, readjusting, and creating again. There is no perfect solution for everything. Within our communities, whether they reach across town or across the continent, we know this: by connecting on a common and engaging level, we go beyond just providing a service. We build relationships to stand the test of time which can weather any storm.

We are proud to be a part of the trucking and CDL operator's community.

And we hope you are too!

Thank you for being part of this foundational and vital industry. It started over a hundred years ago, and the industry promises to be around for at least a hundred years more. We don't know what innovations and technology will affect our industry, but as long as there's a need for long-haulers and drivers, there will be long-haulers here to do the job.

If you feel this book lived up to its promise and delivered more than you hoped for, we'd appreciate a favorable review. By sharing your positive reviews, this important information will rank higher in the lists, increase readership of like-minded drivers, and create a better informed industry and lifestyle for us all.

Thank you!

Special Bonus Offer: Free Gift for You! :)

CDL Business Productivity GAME PLAN

Entrepreneurs Guide to Quick Start your Business to the Next Level

Thank you! Here's a Free Gift! For You :)

As a special thanks from me to you, you'll receive:

- ❏ 3 Powerful Elements of Productivity in your Business
- ❏ 5 Simple Strategies to Mastering Productivity in your Business
- ❏ The Highest Quality of Productivity Charts
- ❏ Valuable Resources that you Must Know and much more!

To receive your Free copy of the CDL Business Productivity GAME PLAN, you can go to my website at:
cdlforlife.com/cdl-business-resources

SCAN ME　　　　　　　　　　　**SCAN ME**
(For your Free Business Game Plan)　　(If you want my Books for Free)

Also If you would like to get my books for Free and before anyone else, go to my website at:
cdlforlife.com/cdl-business-resources

ADDITIONAL INFORMATION, HELPFUL INDUSTRY LINKS, SUGGESTED READING

Forums, Directories, and Online Communities

    Class A Drivers - live forum

    Expeditersonline

    Team Run Smart - Freightliner

    Truckers Report

    Trucking Truth

Marketing Tools and Templates

    12 Free Marketing Budget Templates

    Software Designed Especially for Truckers

Publication Sources for Periodicals and Magazines

WebWire Publications

Samples of Good Trucking Business and Marketing Plans

B Plans

Profitable Venture - Sample Trucking Company Marketing Plan

Support, Advice, and Information Articles for CDL Business Operators

ATBS

Commercial Capital LLC USA and Canada

Trade Shows, Conferences, and Social Events - *event information may be out of date due to the coronavirus (COVID-19). Confirm details with event organizers*

Drivewyze Trucking Events, Trade Shows, and Conferences

Triumph Business Capital Events List

Apps to Help You Do Your Job *Better & Effectively* with Ease

The following apps are available in Google Play Store and Apply Store, unless otherwise stated.

This app gives you the ability to log in your pre-trip, post trip, and driving hours:

Samsara Driver

This app enables you to track your fleet of vehicles your drivers are using:

Samsara Administrator - Fleet

The following two apps are for pre-trip and post-trip inspections to help drivers of small businesses and start-ups save costs and time:

DVIR 2.0 Pre-Trip Inspection

Keep Truckin' Driver - ELD

(The following are ratings and opinions by Smart Trucking - Great Apps for Truckers and More[1], Smart Trucking, who also conducted the testing.)

Whether you are on the road or in the office, we all can use an extra hand now and then.

Well, these aren't extra hands, but they certainly can make your life a bit easier, by either giving you more time, supporting your business, or entertaining you along the way.

All these apps have been tested, both on Android and iPhone devices. Not all of these apps are specifically for drivers, but if they aren't, rest assured, after our test we thought they would be of great benefit. Ratings are on a 5-star system, and none of these listed are below a 4-star rating. They all can be found on both the Apple Store and the Google Play Store.

JOE RYDER

If you find one or several to not be of your liking, please consider, we've done our best to give you some great stuff. If it (they) aren't great or the app isn't available, please delete, but don't hold us accountable. These apps are updated and change often - what was good today may not be worth 2¢ tomorrow!

BEST ALL IN ONE TRUCKER APP
TRUCKER PATH

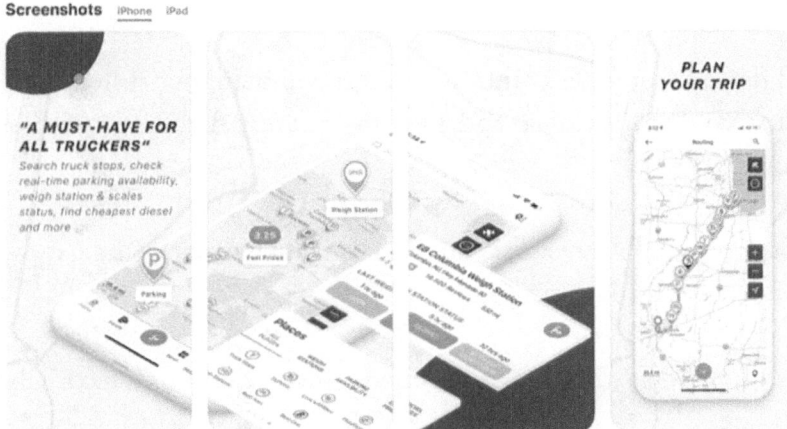

- Lists more than 7000 truck stops in the USA and Canada

- Updates on parking availability

- Truck drivers' forum

- Information on weigh station and scales

- Trip planner option

- Plenty of job listings

- Find fuel stops with truck clearance

- Saves your navigation history

- Helps to find your next truck

- Advanced address search

Trucker Plus has a user-friendly interface and it gives you all the relevant information you would expect.

The Trucker Path comes with a unique mapping system you can use to avoid low bridges and find the nearest fuel stops with truck clearance.

It shows the nearest parking locations including, Walmarts, where you can often park overnight.

You can use the app to compare fuel prices and record hours of service.

You can check on weigh stations and scales.

What makes Trucker Path different from most trucking apps is its huge community; it has more than 800,000 active users in North America. You can chat with other drivers on the truck forum, apply for truck driving jobs, and even search for trucks for sale.

NOTE: The navigation on Trucker Path is not as advanced, compared to specialized GPS units. It can plan routes and find good gas prices, but precise navigation details are not the best-selling points. Stay with the premium GPS units. It also needs internet connections to navigate.

CDL MINDED MARKETING

BEST TRUCKER FUEL APP
GAS BUDDY

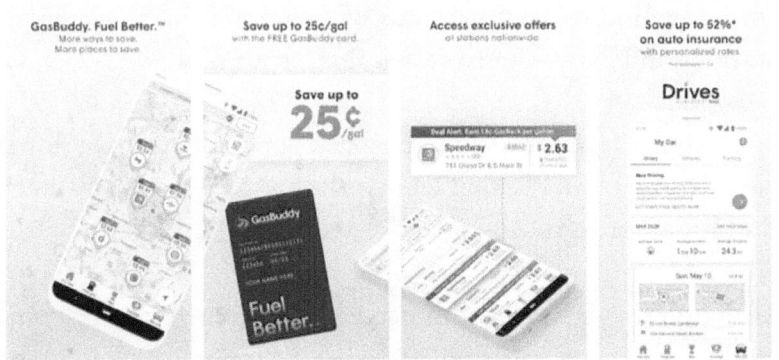

- Includes more than 150,000 gas stations in North America

- Helps to find the cheapest fuel price

- Offers fuel rewards

- Access gas station and store review

- It tells you when you're wasting fuel

- Information on fuel stops with shower and food

Gas Buddy is a free app available on both Android and iPhone.

With a database listing of more than 150,000 fuel stations across North America, finding the cheapest fuel prices is easy.

This app notifies you when the price of diesel is about to increase, so you can fill up your tank before it happens.

It can also monitor your driving habits and inform you when you're wasting gas and money.

Since GasBuddy has thousands of users, you can find reviews for fuel stations and convenience stores along your route.

You may be rewarded with free gas coupons if you pay for items at Walmart, Amazon, Home Depot, or other major retailers using the GasBuddy app or card.

Although Gas Buddy is technically a fuel-saving app, it can inform you where to find fuel stops with food and showers.

CDL MINDED MARKETING

BEST SATELLITE AND STREET VIEWS APP
GOOGLE MAPS

Maps - Navigate & Explore
Google LLC   Travel & Local
3+
Contains Ads
Add to Wishlist
Editors' Choice
★★★★ 11,682,364
Install

 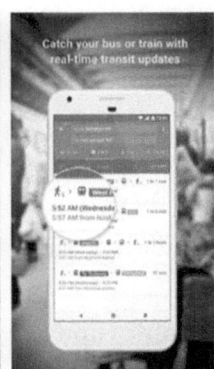 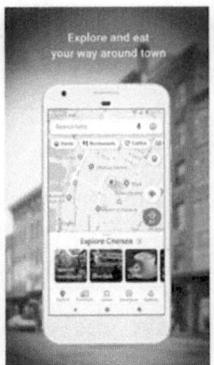 

- Panorama street view

- Satellite view to check parking spots

- Real-time traffic updates

- Updates on businesses that are open and closed

- Discover restaurants, fuel stations, and rest areas

- Saves your search history

- Voice assistance feature (important for truck drivers)

Google Maps is not really an exclusive trucker app, but the satellite and street view feature can be amazingly helpful.

The satellite view allows you to see a property from an overhead position, giving you a heads up on any obstructions, so you will know which driveway to follow, and where to find the dock.

You can switch to street-view easily, to get a 360-degree angle view of different locations on the map, just as you would see it if you're driving on the road in your truck.

Google Maps makes it possible for you to see exactly how a location looks before you arrive at the destination, eliminating any surprises.

You can receive real-time traffic updates and discover points of interest.

In case you're wondering, you can activate voice assistance to give you directions while your eyes are focused on the road (where they belong!) This app doesn't prioritize truck routes.

BEST PRECLEARANCE APP
DRIVEWYZE

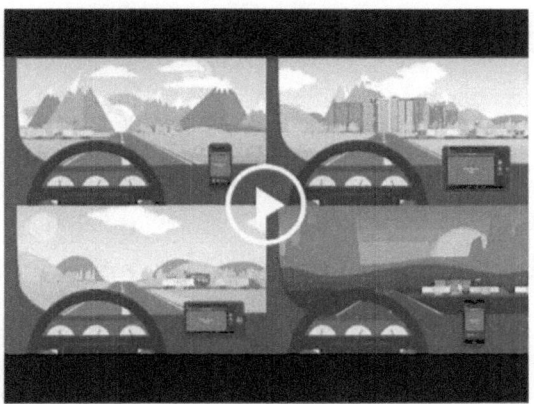

- Helps you to bypass weigh stations

- Approved by over 40 states in the USA

- 30-day free trial

- Receive alerts when you're close to an inspection site or a weigh station

- User-friendly interface How much time do you waste on an inspection site or a weigh station?

On average, 30 minutes to an hour can be wasted on a single weigh station.

The Drivewyze app allows you to legally bypass weigh stations. The company behind it has a preclearance network of at least 700 sites across 44 states and provinces of the United States, and Canada.

If you're using a transponder bypass system, you can integrate it with the app and you will receive alerts at least 2 miles away from inspection sites and weigh stations that have a green-light both your transponder service and Drivewyze.

The app runs in the background and it doesn't require constant interaction, so you can concentrate on driving.

Not all inspection sites and weigh stations are connected to its network, though you will still receive an alert whenever you're near an inspection site or weigh station.

Drivewyze monthly subscription fee is $17.99 but you can get a free trial for the first 30 days. Certainly worth a try to see if it makes your life easier as a truck driver.

PREPASS MOTION

- Pre-clearance for weigh stations

- Helps to save fuel and money

- The app can be paired with a transponder

- Wide network coverage

- Fast customer care

The PrePass Motion is an alternative to Drivewyze, and can be used for pre-clearance purposes.

According to PrePass Motion, the app integrates with the in-cab transponder and Advance Vehicle Identification (AVI) reader, so you can continue driving on the main road without stopping at a weigh scale (this is an untested feature).

If you come across a weigh station without transponder readers, the app uses motion mobile sensors to receive and send the signals.

PrePass MOTION pre-clearance network is available in 42 states across the USA, including Alaska.

Additionally, in California, you can bypass 37 weigh stations and inspection sites using the app.

Users enjoy a toll payment service in most states.

Like Drivewyze, you won't get a pass in all weigh stations nationwide.

It doesn't cover Canada, if you cross the border.

It's free service up to some point, but if you want to enjoy certain privileges, you have to pay the subscription fees.

CDL MINDED MARKETING

BEST MOBILE SCANNING APP
TRANSFLO MOBILE

- You can chat with dispatch

- Accept or decline loads

- Find trailer location

- Tells you weather conditions

- Updates the fuel stops and rest areas along your route

- Mobile scanning option

- It alerts when you approach a weigh station

- Supports hours of service

- Notifies you of payments made

Transflo Mobile is one of the best mobile scanning apps in the trucking industry; although technically, it does more than just scan, send, and receive documents.

You can chat back and forth with your carrier, dispatcher, or broker on the app.

You have an option to reject or accept loads. Once you arrive at your destination, you can confirm pick up delivery via the app.

Fleet managers who have installed T-Series ELD devices on trucks and trailers can use the app to track their location on the map.

Moreover, the app can track when the truck is moving so it can automatically record the hours of service, though to do that, it still needs to be integrated with the T-Series ELD devices.

As soon as you finish a job, collect the needed signatures, take a picture of the documents, and submit it for billing, all through the app. Since you're sending the paperwork on your smartphone, you will be paid faster.

After the payment comes through, the Transflo Mobile app will notify you. Beyond that, you can send photos when reporting an accident or OS&D submission to carriers.

The app can also alert you when approaching a weigh station and show you the fuel stops and rest areas along your route.

Once again, it doesn't navigate better than a dedicated truck GPS. But if you want to scan documents, it will do the job just fine.

BEST TRIP PLANNING APP
PILOT FLYING J

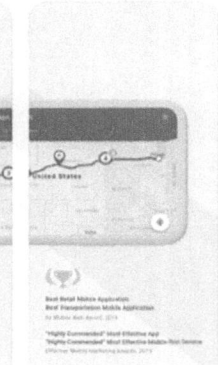

- Free shower rewards

- Access to parking spaces

- Reserve your shower spot at a location

- Free meal on your birthday

- Redeem your points for discounts

- Free drink after signing up

- Reserve a parking spot

- Saves digital receipts

- Mobile fueling option

- Information on available amenities

Before the Pilot Flying J app was launched, the team behind it did a survey and asked many professional truckers what they would like in an app to help their road planning become easier.

Interestingly, most truckers said they would enjoy a free shower; and even if their shower credit expires, they shouldn't worry about it too much.

The outcome was a trip planning app that offers members free daily shower rewards after redeeming re-fueling points.

Otherwise, you can reserve your shower and parking spot using the app, so you avoid wasting time if you're in a hurry (which is more likely than not the case for a truck driver)!

For what it's worth, most Pilot and Flying J locations have reasonably clean showers.

You will get offers and discounts every time you pass through their truck stops. Buy one, get one free, or maybe free coffee. Did I mention, you get a free meal on your birthday?

You can use the mobile fueling option to fill out the fuel pump prompts in advance. In addition, the app shares information about the amenities available at nearby locations. It can tell you what type of food is available, the number of parking spots open, number of showers, and truck assistance services in specified locations.

You can, however, only access those free showers, parking spots, and special discounts at Pilot and Flying J locations. With 750 Pilot Flying J locations across North America, though, it isn't too hard to find one enroute.

CDL MINDED MARKETING

LOVE'S CONNECT

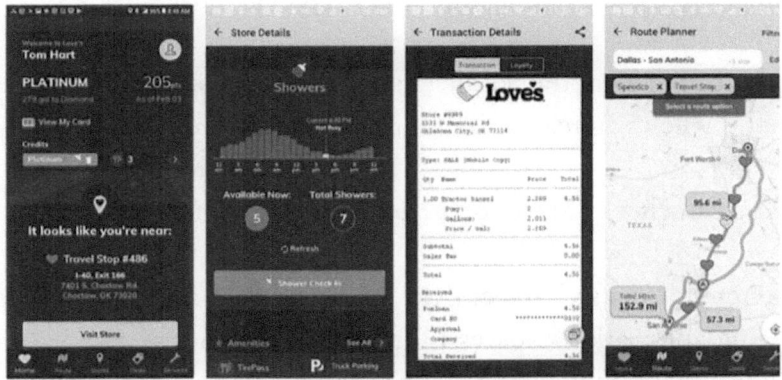

- Helps locate the nearest LOVE'S truck stop

- You can redeem points for rewards

- It saves digital receipts

- Check fuel prices along your route

- Activate the pump from your phone

- Shower check-in feature

If you prefer a different trip planning app than Pilot Flying J, Love's Connect is a good alternative; maybe you can use both.

You can use the app to get location pins on the nearest Love's truck stops.

Once you arrive at any Love's travel stop, you can book a shower slot using your smartphone.

You will receive points after every refuel at Love's truck stops.

You can redeem the points to shop for items or free showers. Keep in mind, when you reach Platinum status, *your points will triple.*

You can check for competitive fuel prices along your route.

Though Love's Connect ticks almost all the boxes for the best trip planning app, parking spaces fill up fast. Customer service will make you a priority, though, if you use the app.

BEST AUDIOBOOK APP
AUDIBLE

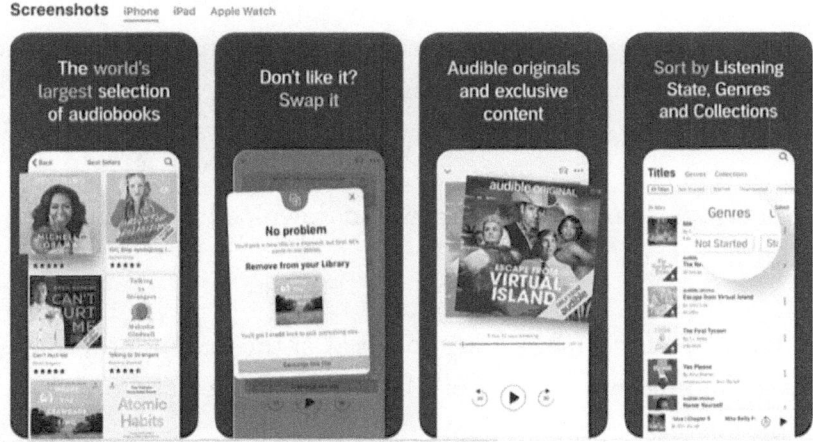

- Wide collection of audiobooks

- Customize your library

- Listen to audiobooks offline

- Sign in with Amazon account

- User-friendly interface

- Free first-month trial

If you want to listen to audiobooks in your truck, Audible gives you access to thousands of titles.

Users sign in with their Amazon account. If you're a new member, you receive a 30-day free trial.

After the free trial expires, your account will be billed $14.95 per month. However, if you're an Amazon Prime member, you will receive discounts and free Audible content.

For easy navigation, the content is categorized into different genres and collections. You also have access to the 'bestseller' lists for the New York Times, Amazon, etc.

You can personalize your library and download the audiobooks to listen offline.

You won't receive many free goodies after the first month, but considering Audible has the world's largest catalog of audiobooks, the subscription fees seem reasonable.

www.ingramcontent.com/pod-product-compliance
Lightning Source LLC
Chambersburg PA
CBHW031630210526
45464CB00004B/1835

BEST MUSIC STREAMING APP
SPOTIFY

- Good audio quality

- Create your playlist

- Easy to search interface

- Integrate with other devices

- Free version available

Spotify is the biggest music streaming service at the moment with a catalog of more than 50 million songs and 700,000 podcasts. Its huge library makes it perfect to listen to music on the road without getting bored.

Users can choose the free version available with adverts or the premium version with no ads.

As might be expected, there is a 1-month free trial if you have never paid for premium.

You can access Spotify on any device with Windows, Android, macOS, and iOS. You can also create playlists. If you choose to discontinue your premium membership, you will lose access to your playlists and any content you may have downloaded.

BEST APP FOR RELAXATION
CALM RADIO

- Lots of music channels

- Meditation music

- Sleep timer

- Equalizer tone controls

- Nature sounds in the background

- Unlimited listening

- Free membership with ads

This app is convenient when you're on a break and you probably want to sleep or meditate. You know, recharge your batteries before the next trip?

The app comes with more than 500 HD audio channels to stream relaxation music. If you want a free membership, the channels will have ads, a bit disturbing if you are in the middle of a meditation. Otherwise, you'll need to pay a slight membership fee, which is very worth it.

Besides listening to all types of relaxing genres like Jazz, classical music, country music, pop-rock, and adult contemporary, you can choose to play nature sounds in the background, which are very true to life. You feel like you are at the beach or in the forest. Better yet, you can listen to binaural beat therapy and set up a sleep timer.

This is one of my favorite apps and is quite reasonably priced for the premium version if you watch for their occasional deals (I paid $70 CDN for an entire year). Excellent value.

CDL MINDED MARKETING

BEST FITNESS APP FOR TRUCKERS
ROLLING STRONG

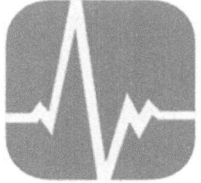

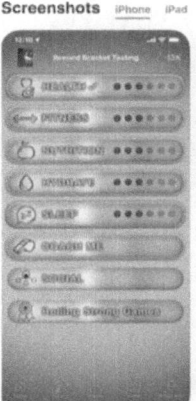  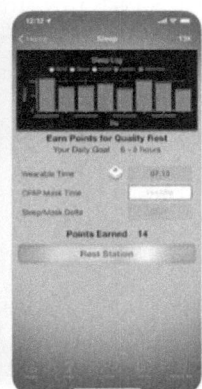 

- It tells you nearest fitness spots

- Monitors your sleeping pattern

- Helps track your calories

- Redeem points for rewards

- Online coaching to get fit

- Reminds you to hydrate

Once you sign up to the app, its AI will guide you to create a diet and a workout plan to fit your goals.

Beyond that, the app will monitor your sleeping pattern and remind you when it's time to hydrate.

Since you will be on the road frequently, the app will show you the nearest fitness spots with truck parking spaces available based on your locations. Alternatively, you can watch exercise training videos and consult with fitness coaches through the app to help you work out if you can't find a gym.

To enjoy the full perks of the Rolling Strong app, you need to pay a monthly membership fee of $4.99. That's cheap for a fitness app with an assistant coach.

In a nutshell, all the apps on this list are ideal for truck drivers and compatible with Android and iPhones. Of course, you don't need to clutter your smartphone with too many apps, just use the ones you think you will benefit from.

Above everything else, keep your hands away from the phone when you're driving. If you must engage an app when you're at the wheel, make sure your smartphone is mounted on the dashboard and you can activate voice assistance.

SUGGESTED READING

Progressive Business Plan for an Independent Trucking Company: A Detailed Template System with Innovative Growth Strategies

Setting up an independent trucking company is heavily dependent on having the right plan and a strategic vision. These are the aspects of a business setup that the book will address.

Online Advertising Made Simple - Trucking

The focus here is specifically on digital marketing and how it could be beneficial for a trucking or CDL company.

CDL Minded Entrepreneur: 3-Step System to Leverage Time, Have Unlimited Freedom and Maximize Security in the CDL Industry

This book provides excellent guidance and the overall CDL mindset on starting and building a successful business.

REFERENCES

[1] MacMillan, C. *The best trucker apps 2020 – for on + off the road.* Smart Trucking. https://www.smart-trucking.com/trucker-apps/

[2] Truckernews.com. Truckers favor Facebook which turns 15 today. https://www.truckersnews.com/survey-truckers-favor-facebook-which-turns-15-today/

[3] Bureau of Labor Statistics. News release. National census of fatal occupational injuries in 2018. 12/17/2019. https://www.bls.gov/news.release/pdf/cfoi.pdf

[10] Best Web Hosting Services. (2020). https://hostingfacts.com/

[11] Best Free Website Builders. (2020). https://www.websitebuilderexpert.com/website-builders/best/free/

Thank you for your Honest Experience :)

Thank you! I hope this brings you great value as it did for me sharing my story with you.

My purpose and mission is to guide and encourage you to become the best version of yourself in your life by providing everything you need to achieve your dreams for yourself, your family and your business.

However, in order to do that, sharing your honest review on **amazon** (or Audible) helps spread the word to other CDL Minded friends (like yourself) and will help many readers who are struggling to make their dreams become a reality.

If you do have 30 secs to leave a **1-Click honest review,** I greatly appreciate it because it shows that you're not like most people.

It means that you truly value yourself in what you do. It also means that you're CDL Minded in yourself, your family and in your business.

I truly appreciate all your love and support and I'm thankful and grateful for your life and I greatly value your honest opinion and thoughts. :)

If you need anything, feel free to reach out at my website and to receive your Free Gift if you haven't received it yet.

You can also share your experience by taking a photo of this book and attach it to the review so other CDL Minded friends can be inspired and encouraged from your honest experience.

SCAN ME!

Just One Click (once you click on this review page or scan QR Code):

When you finish, just Click Submit at the bottom of the page and that's it. Please click on this link or scan the QR code to **Review Book on Amazon!**

Looking forward to working together and helping you achieve your goals. Take care and talk to you soon! :)